HOUSE OF THRILLS:

The History of Forbes Field and the
Development of Oakland

I0555194

Douglas R. Spear

To my mother and father, for their constant love and support.

ACKNOWLEDGMENTS

Throughout the past nine months, many people have assisted me in my studies of Forbes Field and the Oakland section of the city of Pittsburgh. The staff at the Special Collections department of the Hillman Library at the University of Pittsburgh was extremely helpful and patient with my many demands. Corey Seeman at the Historical Society of Western Pennsylvania provided me with sources on Pittsburgh history, as well as someone with whom I could share my ideas while at home. Marilyn Holt at the Carnegie Library's Pennsylvania Department was a godsend from day one, pointing me toward sources, communicating with me via email, and giving me access to all of the library's available resources. Sally O'Leary of the Pittsburgh Pirates opened her files to me and served as a wonderful source of sources.

Tom Johnson provided me with the Pirates' perspective on the sale of Forbes Field, Dr. Jack Freeman explained the University of Pittsburgh's perspective on its destruction, and Art McKennan brought me back in time so that I might know what it was like to grow up near Forbes Field in its early years. To these gentlemen, and to the other men and women who took the time to speak with me about places and times I never knew, I am most grateful.

Dr. Bruce Kuklick has advised me on this project since I developed the idea in March 1994. He has made himself available to me, read and critiqued every word of this thesis, and provided me with the kind of guidance that only he could give. Without his help, this paper would still be an Independent Study in waiting.

Although I never had the pleasure of seeing Forbes Field, I am lucky to have a father who spent many summer days there watching Ralph Kiner hit home runs and could share with me stories about his favorite place. His father, my grandfather, gave me a program and a ticket from the 1960 World Series, still the greatest sports event in the history of Pittsburgh. These items, along with the seats from the ballpark that my mother purchased before it was destroyed, and that sat idly in our backyard for years, served as a constant reminder of Forbes Field.

To anyone who has never seen Forbes Field and believes it was just a place where people played games, I hope this makes you think again. And, to those who remember Oakland and its ballpark, picture what once was, and smile.

ABOUT THE AUTHOR

Douglas R. Spear is a partner at the law firm of Nelson Mullins, where he serves as co-chair of the firm's corporate group. He is a graduate of the University of Pennsylvania and earned his law degree from the University of Pittsburgh School of Law. He maintains a prominent presence within startup communities across the southeastern United States and beyond. Mr. Spear is highly regarded for his legal practice, particularly in the representation of technology and software startups. Douglas R. Spear was raised in Pittsburgh and continues to be a devoted supporter of the Pittsburgh Pirates. This book originated as his undergraduate dissertation. He resides in Atlanta, Georgia, with his wife, Andrea, and they are the parents of three daughters.

TABLE OF CONTENTS

Introduction...1

Chapter 1: Pirate Baseball –The Early Years 6

Chapter 2: Birth Of Oakland..17

Chapter 3: A New Home 29

Chapter 4: A Place For All People................................... 47

Chapter 5: Triumph, Tragedy, Technology 61

Chapter 6: The Golden Era? 88

Chapter 7: Times Of Change: Pitt And The Renaissance
.... 106

Chapter 8: How Sweet It Is! 125

Chapter 9: Farewell...139

Chapter Notes... 161

Critical Bibliography 175

Selected Bibliography...187

INTRODUCTION

As I sat in Art McKennan's apartment on the afternoon of August 13, 1994, I began to understand. I was there to interview him, so that I could learn about Forbes Field and life in Oakland in the early twentieth century. As he spoke, I marvelled at his background. He was born in 1906 and raised on Dawson Street in the Oakland section of Pittsburgh. A few blocks from his home stood Forbes Field, the home of the Pittsburgh Pirates from 1909-1970. As a young boy, Art McKennan played near the ballpark and enjoyed going to games there with his father. As a teen, he was allowed to attend games by himself, using a quarter his father gave him to purchase a ticket after school in the spring. In the summertime, McKennan ran errands for the players at Forbes Field while they practiced and became familiar with the team and the ballpark. He ushered in the 1925 World Series, began to assist in operating the scoreboard in 1927, but came down with polio in 1930. However, twelve years later, McKennan was operating the scoreboard again, and in 1948, a public address system was installed at the ballpark. Fittingly, he was chosen to operate it, which he did so well until the park closed in 1970. Then, he moved with the team to Three Rivers Stadium and worked there until he retired in 1989. Art McKennan had been involved with Pittsburgh Pirates baseball forever, it seemed.

While the story of Mr. McKennan's life was interesting and unique, it was not what brought me to him that day. I wanted to learn more about Forbes Field and had been told that he knew it better than anyone. He told me about the ballpark in great detail, reinforcing some of the information I had read earlier, and supplementing it with his own descriptions. We discussed the events that occurred inside the park, such as baseball games, boxing matches, and remodeling, and those that occurred outside, such as the development of Schenley Park, the growth of Oakland as a commercial center, and the rise of the University of Pittsburgh. Mr. McKennan lived in Oakland for much of his life and was a witness to the area's changes,

I was struck by McKennan's admiration for the ballpark and his memory of the events that took place there. Our conversation remained unemotional until I asked him to discuss the sale of Forbes Field and its eventual closing. I sensed his love for the ballpark earlier, but was moved by his final memories of Forbes Field.

"The last night before they (the Pirates) got out of there, I remember stopping after coming downstairs from my booth, hours after the crowd had left. I remember looking at all those empty seats, beautifully symmetrical, and I felt like staying there all night, and sitting up there like I was sitting up with a friend who was dying...I grew up with that park, and it felt so bad."

As I listened to McKennan's comments, I began to understand that Forbes Field was more than just a ballpark to anyone lucky enough to know it. Through various other interviews, books, articles, and stories, I came to realize the importance of Forbes Field to the people of Pittsburgh, in particular to those living in Oakland. Forbes Field was known as the home of the sports teams of Living Pittsburgh, but meant much more to those who lived, worked, and played near it.

Forbes Field was the center of entertainment and activity in Oakland since its construction in 1909. Although it was preceded in the area by some developments, it gave rise to tremendous growth in Oakland and brought people into the community. Through the years, Oakland blossomed into Pittsburgh's most popular neighborhood, only to become engulfed by the University of Pittsburgh. While many changes occurred in Oakland throughout the twentieth century, Forbes Field remained impervious to change. By 1970, Oakland had changed dramatically, but the ballpark still stood as a reminder of its past.

What follows is a history of Forbes Field and Oakland. It is a story of urban growth and modernization. It is a story of a baseball team, of champions and cellar-dwellers. It is a story of people and places, of ethnic diversity and good times. It is a story of the growth of the importance of education and medicine in American society. It is a story of young boys attending games with their fathers, of children scaling walls, and of rolling hills and ivy-covered walls. It is a story of a ballpark, a community, and an everlasting love affair between the two. It is a story of the House of Thrills.

CHAPTER 1: PIRATE BASEBALL –

THE EARLY YEARS

The earliest signs of organized baseball in Pittsburgh appeared immediately following the Civil War. Al Pratt, a Union officer, returned home in 1866 and put together an amateur team known as the Pittsburgh Enterprise Club[1]. Over the ensuing ten years, several more amateur teams were formed as baseball became popular in the Steel City and throughout the nation. In 1876, the Pittsburgh public's interest in baseball became so great that a club was organized to play for money. This team, the first professional one in Western Pennsylvania, was to be called the Alleghenies. Soon, the team was asked to become a member of the newly formed International Association[2]. Their first game was played at Union Park in Old Allegheny City on April 15, 1876, as they defeated the Pittsburgh Xanthas, 7-3. The team's success was short-lived, however, as many of the Alleghenies' better players jumped to teams in other leagues that were forming across the country. The International League soon fizzled, as did professional baseball in Pittsburgh.

The most formidable league, the National League, awarded a franchise to the Pittsburgh Alleghenies ten years later, in 1887, after the Kansas City club was removed due to its distance from the other Eastern clubs. The team played its home games at Recreation Park, located along the Fort Wayne Railroad and the Allegheny River. The team became known as the Pirates due to the circumstances surrounding the signing of infielder Louis Bierbauer in 1893. The American Association protested the acquisition, claiming that Bierbauer belonged to it. An arbitrator ruled in favor of the Pittsburgh club, but an Association spokesman said, "The action of the Pittsburgh club in signing Bierbauer was piratical".[3] Thus, the nickname "Pirates" was born, and eventually became the official team name. The highest finish for the team occurred in 1893, as they came in second behind the Boston club. In 1895, the Pirates' owner, Bill "Captain" Kerr, named his catcher as the team's new manager. Cornelius McGillicuddy, better known as Connie Mack, managed the team for two and a half seasons, as the Pirates finished at the bottom of the league.[4] In fact, the Pirates would close the decade as a tenant of the second division (a term used to describe the lower half of the league standings). A lack of talent caused the fans to become disinterested in the team, and a jump-start was needed.

The poor performances of the Pittsburgh club would soon change with the entrance of a dynamic German immigrant. Barney Dreyfuss, born in Freiburg in 1866, emigrated to the United States at the age of 17[5]. He arrived at MAGARA at Castle Garden in New York's Battery Park, and headed for Niagara Falls, a place he had read much about in his German school books[6]. Soon, Dreyfuss would reach his final destination of Paducah, Kentucky, where he had several relatives. He did not speak any English, but obtained his first job cleaning whiskey barrels at the Bernheim Distillery in Paducah for $6 a week[7]. In time, Dreyfuss improved his English and was promoted to an office position in the distillery, eventually becoming the head bookkeeper. His rise within the organization was not without its difficulties, though, as Dreyfuss's work habits drove him to poor health. The nine-hour workday, coupled with his studies of English at night, caused the frail Dreyfuss to suffer from headaches and other maladies. A doctor in Paducah admonished Dreyfuss for "not getting any recreation or fun out of life." He ordered Dreyfuss to become involved in outdoor activities.

Barney Dreyfuss took an early interest in the American game of baseball. Taking the doctor's advice, he organized a semi-pro team in Paducah and even dabbled at second base for the club. Still, the distillery occupied most of Dreyfuss' time, and when it moved to Louisville in 1888, he naturally went along. Louisville was a much larger city than Paducah, and already had a professional baseball team. The club played in the American Association, which was supported mainly by owners of breweries and distilleries. Dreyfuss continued to be captivated by baseball, and soon purchased a small block of stock from the Louisville owner, George

Ruckstool. By 1890, Dreyfuss was elected treasurer of the club, which was admitted to the dominant National League shortly thereafter. Eventually, Dreyfuss obtained control of the team and emphasized finishing in the "first division," a term used to describe the best 6 (later 4) teams in the league.

The financial success of the Louisville club was largely dependent upon Sunday crowds. The prevailing sentiment among the owners of National League clubs in large cities was to decrease the size of the league. Andy Freedman, the owner of the New York Giants, attempted to force Dreyfuss' Louisville club into bankruptcy by creating a schedule with no Sunday games. Fortunately for Barney, Joe Vila, a sportswriter for the New York Morning Sun, got word of the plan. Vila stole the proposed schedule from the coat pocket of A.H. Soden, owner of the Boston club and Chairman of the Schedule Committee, at the bar in the Fifth Avenue Hotel in New York. Vila printed a copy of the schedule in the next morning's paper, and Freedman's plot to ruin the Louisville club had been documented. After reading the article, Dreyfuss, his English still poor, created such a fuss at the owner's meeting the next day that Freedman and Soden agreed to give him the full quota of Sunday games.

Dreyfuss was lucky enough to thwart this initial attempt to eliminate his club, but his luck began to disappear in the winter of 1899-90. Receipts at the gate were down in Louisville, and the club's home field had just burned down. Harry Pulliam, the Secretary of the Louisville club and Dreyfuss's close friend, had gotten word of the National League's plan to cut the four "deadwood" teams from its membership: Cleveland, Washington, Baltimore, and Louisville. Alter Dreyfuss realized that the move was inevitable, so he gathered money from his savings to purchase another club. Ile wanted to stay in baseball, both because he loved the game and saw tremendous profits in its future.

John Brush, the owner of the Cincinnati club and a friend of Pulliam's, alerted Dreyfuss about the possibilities in Pittsburgh. That club, owned by Bill "Captain" Kerr, was losing money at an alarming rate.

Dreyfuss went to Pittsburgh in the winter of 1900 to meet Kerr and came away with a half-interest in the Pittsburgh club. Knowing his Louisville team would soon fold, Dreyfuss agreed to a deal that clearly favored his new team. He sent fourteen members of the Louisville club to Pittsburgh in exchange for five Pirates and $525,000 cash. The deal, considered one of the most lopsided in baseball history, brought instant credibility to the struggling Pittsburgh club. Included in the set of Louisville players headed to Pittsburgh were stars such as outfielder and manager Fred Clarke, utility man Honus Wagner, shortstop Tommy Leach, and pitchers Deacon Phillipe and Rube Waddell. Jack Cheshro, a star pitcher traded by the Pirates to Louisville, returned to Pittsburgh when the Louisville team folded. A dynasty was about to begin in Pittsburgh.

The 1900 season showed the promise of the Pirates' future. Honus Wagner, the gem of the Louisville deal, won the first of his eight batting titles with a 380 average. Fred Clarke and Ginger Beaumont were both feared hitters and strong outfielders for the club. Clarke doubled as the team's manager, often providing rowdy tactics that drew more fans to watch the team play in Exposition Park. Dreyfuss helped to keep the payroll to a modest $36,000 that Mason, as National League rules placed a ceiling of $2,400 on any player's salary.

After the season, Dreyfuss acquired the remaining stock from Kerr and his partners. While Ban Johnson's upstart American League began to emerge as a competitor by snatching players away from National League clubs, Dreyfuss was able to keep his team intact. His 1901 club took over first place on June 16 and won their first pennant. This season was also marked by Ginger Beaumont's batting title, but his accomplishments were overshadowed by the move of Honus Wagner to Shortstop. Wagner was originally an outfielder and first baseman for the Pirates. His move to the infield was prompted by rumors that the current shortstop, Ely, was considering leaving for a team in the AL. Upon hearing of this possibility, Dreyfuss fined and benched Ely and ordered Clarke to place Tommy Leach at shortstop, moving Wagner to third base. After one week, Clarke asked the two men to switch positions after Leach hurt his knee and had less range, and appeared a genius as Wagner went on to become arguably the greatest shortstop to ever play the game.

The Pirates went on to win the National League Pennant each of the next two seasons. After the 1903 season, newspapers across the country demanded that the Pirates, as champions of the NL, play the Boston Pilgrims, champions of the AL., to determine the true "world" champion. Many of the National League owners felt it was unnecessary to play the champion of the upstart league, citing the fact that they had nothing to gain by the contest.[10] Dreyfuss disagreed with his peers, and Boston owner Harry J. Killilea came to Pittsburgh to make the arrangements. A best-of-nine game series was chosen as the forum for the match-up, the first three to be played in Boston.

The Pirates defeated the Pilgrims 7-3, as Jimmy Sebring hit the first home run in World Series history and Deacon Phillippe outdueled the legendary Cy Young. The Pilgrims shut the Pirates out the next day to even the series. 18,000 fans jammed Boston's Huntington Avenue grounds for the third game, as Pittsburgh garnered the victory. Fred Clarke called on Phillippe to pitch with little rest, yet he stifled the Boston batters again, 4-2. With a two games to one lead, the series headed back to Pittsburgh for the next four games.

The Pirates were confident that they could finish the series in Pittsburgh. Honus Wagner, echoing the sentiments of his teammates, said, "No use dragging it out any longer than we have to. I don't want to go back to Boston. I got some hunting I want to do." Phillippe pitched for the Pirates and won again, despite a disappointing crowd of only 7,600 at Exposition Park. Young pitched well in game five as Boston won 11-2, and Boston also won game six to even the series. In game 7, 17,600 fans jammed into Exposition Park to watch Young battle Phillippe again. This time, the Pilgrims won 7-3 and headed back to Boston one game away from winning the first World Series. Boston's Dineen shut the Pirates out, 8-0, as the Pilgrims won the eighth game and the series.

The Pirates' pitching troubles that became so evident during the series proved to be their downfall for the next four seasons. Although they continued to finish in the first division, the National League pennant eluded Dreyfuss after 1903. Despite Wagner's batting titles in 1904, 1906, and 1907, the team's pitching remained inconsistent. In 1908, the Pirates nearly won the pennant but fell to the Chicago Cubs on the final day of the season. After that game, Barney Dreyfuss said, "Only one team could win, and it wasn't ours." The owner and his team were frustrated after the loss, knowing they had the talent to represent the National League in the World Series as they had six seasons earlier.

CHAPTER 2: BIRTH OF OAKLAND

The city of Pittsburgh is surrounded by steep mountains and water that separates it from its neighbors. It begins at its westernmost edge at the confluence of the Monongahela, Allegheny, and Ohio Rivers. This area, called "the point," was home in 1754 to the French Fort Duquesne in their struggle with the British to control North America. By 1800, Pittsburgh's population was about 45,000, most of whom lived in log houses near or in the downtown area. Over the next forty years, Pittsburgh became an industrial center, producing much of the glass, iron, and oil in the United States. Large groups of immigrants travelled to Pittsburgh in search of work, and found it in the city's many factories, most of which were located downtown or across the Allegheny River in Allegheny City, later called the North Side.

Many people lived near their places of work, so when the "Great Fire" swept through downtown Pittsburgh in 1845, residents were forced to flee the area for the suburbs. One section of the greater region that was largely uninhabited was the suburban Bellefield, the farm covered with Oak trees that belonged to Neville Craig, the editor of the Pittsburgh Gazette, and a few other businessmen[11]. The Dithridge Company, a glass manufacturer, recognized the need for housing away from the charcoaled downtown, so they bought Bellefield, only three miles east of downtown, and constructed homes there. By 1860, passenger rail service had encouraged residential and commercial growth just east of Bellefield, and in 1868, the entire area was officially annexed by the City of Pittsburgh as Oakland[12].

Oakland occupied seven hundred acres in the city atop a plateau nearly three miles from downtown. It was surrounded by the Monongahela River to the south, a gully or hollow to the east, and steep hills to the north and west.

Because it was slightly geographically set apart from the rest of Pittsburgh, Oakland remained somewhat of a rural retreat following its annexation. In fact, in 1873, a hunt was organized to catch a fox that was causing a disturbance in Oakland's chicken houses[13]. Much of this rural territory was owned by Mary Croghan Schenley, the inheritor of the wealthy Croghan and O'Hara estates. Mrs. Schenley eloped to London with a Captain in the British army and lived in England despite her enormous properties in Pittsburgh.

As the city remained crowded and filled with smoke from its many industrial plants, the average man had no place to "breathe." [14] In 1888, Edward Bigelow, the city's Director of Public Works, determined that a public park would be the remedy to this problem. He proposed that the city obtain a large portion of Mrs. Schenley's estate, a four-hundred-thirty-four-acre plot known as the Mount Airy tract, to serve as a public park. This idea was originally proposed in 1869, but city voters rejected the underwriting of a bond proposal to finance the acquisition[15]. Mrs. Schenley conducted her business transactions in Pittsburgh through Robert Carnahan, her lawyer and a member of the City Council. Bigelow faced competition from a real estate syndicate that wished to purchase the tract. However, with Carnahan's assistance, Bigelow was ultimately successful in obtaining it for the city. On October 10, 1889, Mary Schenley gave three hundred acres of Mt. Airy to the City of Pittsburgh to be used as a park. She also sold nineteen acres at the entrance of the tract to the city for $75,000, and another one hundred fifteen acres slightly north of the would-be park to the city for $125,000[16].

Although Bigelow's intention may have been to aid the common man, the park, named after its donor, was initially of use to the wealthy who lived in the suburbs a few miles east of Oakland. The green beauty was inaccessible to the masses of immigrants and the poor, whose dwellings were far from Oakland.

Thus, despite its ability to attract visitors from all over the region, Schenley Park was, in its early years, largely the domain of the affluent.

Another of Mrs. Schenley's trusted associates was Andrew Carnegie, the Pittsburgh steel magnate who amassed his fortune across the Monongahela River from the East End at the Homestead Steel Works. Carnegie became tired of Pittsburgh's reputation as a smoke-filled, corrupt area. Instead, he felt, Pittsburgh should be a place of culture where the leisure class could flourish. Carnegie was able to convince Schenley that a museum, in connection with her beautiful gift to the city, would be a giant step toward creating a center of culture in Pittsburgh. Thus, part of the deed for the sale of Mrs. Schenley's land to the city made provisions for a museum to be located within the park's limits[17].

In 1890, Carnegie purchased 19 acres at the entrance to the park (the same 19 acres sold to the city for $75,000) to build a public library, "free to the people." The construction of the library was delayed because Pittsburgh city officials did not feel they could adequately support the library after Mr. Carnegie's initial gift of $1 million was expended[18]. While he waited for support from the city, Carnegie paid close attention to the World Columbian Exposition in Chicago in 1893. He would use this fair as a model for further development in Oakland. He convinced Henry Phipps, an associate, to build a flower conservatory across St. Pierre Ravine from his library site. The conservatory was the mirror image of Horticultural Hall at the Chicago Expo[19].

By 1895, Carnegie had cleared all political obstacles to his library, and it was constructed similarly to the Newberry Library in Chicago. He also built an adjoining museum and music hall, and the three buildings together became known as the Carnegie Institute. Oakland, first with the park, then the conservatory, and now the Institute, was slowly evolving into more than just a rural area.

Bigelow was determined to give the citizens of Pittsburgh greater access to Schenley Park, so in 1897, he directed the city to build four bridges connecting the park to other areas and crossing the two hollows that engulfed the park. He also added an ice rink, a bandshell, a racetrack, and the artificial Panther Hollow Lake, complete with boating facilities[20]. Still, more attractions were necessary if Oakland was to truly become, as Carnegie hoped, an accepted area by the leisure class.

Andrew Carnegie, though, was not the only person with great dreams for Oakland. Mary Schenley, pleased with her park and the Institute's proximity to it, also had high hopes for the region. However, neither of these individuals had the grand vision for Oakland that was possessed by Franklin Nicola, a real estate developer from Ohio. Nicola had been to Oakland and was impressed with the developments in the area, so much so that he successfully acquired a parcel of land between Forbes and Fifth Avenues, just north of the Institute and the entrance to the park[21]. After acquiring this property, Nicola shared his plan for Oakland with Carnegie. He wanted to build the city's most luxurious hotel on the site, with the hope that he could acquire more of the surrounding land after Mrs. Schenley's death. As one of the executors of her estate, Carnegie knew he could help Nicola acquire more land on which to build, thus increasing the value of his Institute. With Nicola's vision, Oakland could be transformed from a land filled with cow pastures into the place of which Carnegie had always dreamed.

Carnegie shared Nicola's vision for Oakland with some of his wealthier associates and convinced them to financially support Nicola. This effort resulted in the creation of the Bellefield Company, a stock company capitalized with $400,000 from fifty-eight of Pittsburgh's wealthiest people, at $100/share. Carnegie purchased one hundred shares, Mayor Christopher Magee one hundred fifty, George Westinghouse fifty, H.J. Heinz fifty, Nicola one hundred fifty, and even Mary Schenley herself purchased two hundred shares. Many other well-known Pittsburghers invested, making the ownership of the company seem like a "who's who" of the region. These people supported Nicola's vision, and with their help, the luxurious Schenley Hotel, ten stories high, opened in 1898. It would become the "favorite stopover for all the big names that visited the city," and would remain Pittsburgh's finest hotel throughout its existence[22].

By the turn of the century, the park, library, museum, music hall, and hotel were all flourishing. Carnegie had promised Mayor Magee a technical school for the city if he could provide the land on which to build it. Magee came through, providing a lot next to Schenley

Park, across Junction Hollow from the Carnegie Institute, and connecting around to Forbes Avenue. Carnegie initiated a contest to design his school, and Henry Hornbostel was declared the winner in 1903. The original campus was constructed by 1905, again modeled after the Chicago Exposition of 1893, and expanded several times thereafter. Higher education, another institution previously foreign to the area, was now present in Oakland.

Nicola still had higher aspirations for Oakland. In 1905, his Schenley Land Company purchased one hundred three acres of the Schenley Estate from the city (Mrs. Schenley passed away in 1903) for approximately $3 million. This land encompassed a large area bounded by Forbes Avenue on the South, Center Avenue on the North, Bellefield Avenue on the East, and Bouquet Street on the West. Nicola dreamed of Oakland as the model city, with four separate quarters: residential, educational, monumental, and social[23]. The Nicola syndicate began to build streets and laid down a single large conduit for water pipes, gas pipes, and telephone and electric wires[24].

Nicola designated the northernmost section of his land purchase as Schenley Farms, the future residential quarter of Oakland. There, he created a lavish landscape on the hillside, planting trees for shade, and built ninety-six homes in Edwardian domestic style[25]. Nicola referred to his Schenley Farms as a "model community," describing the walls with insulating air chambers, hardwood floors, finished basements, brass pipes, ducts for vacuum cleaning, and stained glass that each home would receive[26]. For $20,000-30,000, these homes were truly a bargain for the wealthy.

The monumental quarter in Nicola's plan began to take shape with a contest to design a memorial for the dead of Allegheny County from the Civil War and other battles. Again, Hornbostel won the contest and began plans to design a grand building on Fifth Avenue. Construction began in 1907, but was not completed until 1911.

While Nicola was still planning the social section of Oakland, he had already conceived the ultimate addition to his educational quarter. Although Carnegie's Technical School was established and operating only minutes from Nicola's property, he desperately hoped that higher education would enter his "community." He had reserved forty-three acres just west of Schenley Farms for the University of Pittsburgh, the city's largest school. It wanted to relocate to Oakland, but preferred the thirteen acres along Forbes Avenue that lay adjacent to the Schenley Hotel. However, Nicola had already sold that property to Henry Frick, so he convinced the University leaders to accept his original offer of land on the hillside. In 1907, they agreed, and for $537,000, the land was theirs[27].

In less than twenty years, Oakland had been transformed from farmland to a budding civic center. Patrons could read their favorite authors at the Carnegie Library, listen to a concert at the music hall, learn about the dinosaurs at the museum, dine at the exquisite restaurant of the Schenley Hotel, or spend a day exploring Schenley Park. Soon, they would be able to live in beautiful homes, have social gatherings at their private clubs, and enjoy the monuments that would rise in Oakland. All of these attractions were within walking distance for those who lived in Oakland, and a short streetcar ride for those coming from downtown or eastern sections of the city. A streetcar barn along Fifth Avenue allowed this form of transportation to be convenient for all. With Nicola's vision, Carnegie's dreams were being realized. For years, Pittsburgh had been targeted by the likes of Lincoln Steffens as the most corrupt and socially repressive city in the United States[28]. Through the development of Oakland, this label was beginning to disappear.

CHAPTER 3: A NEW HOME

Despite the Pirates' exciting finish in 1908, the team did not draw well at the gate. Home attendance that season was only 382,444 over an eighty-one game schedule[29]. The reasons for the low attendance figures lie within the grounds of Exposition Park, the Pirates' home since 1891. The Park was located 50 yards from the banks of the Allegheny River, just north of and across the river from downtown Pittsburgh. There were four major problems with Exposition Park. First, the grandstand was constructed entirely of wood, making it susceptible to fire and rotting. Secondly, its proximity to the Allegheny River made flooding incidents frequent. Barney Dreyfuss once said, "My players need rafts to play their positions. [30]" Games were often cancelled during periods of high rain, and schedules were disrupted. Another negative aspect of Exposition Park was the neighborhood in which it was located. A working-class community, the North Shore of the city was hardly Dreyfuss's choice to be the home of a game as noble as baseball. He once said, "The better class of citizens, especially when accompanied by their womenfolk, were loathe to go there[31]." The most obvious problem at Exposition Park was its size, holding only 17,000 at its capacity, with many people forced to stand. Dreyfuss wanted a larger park in a better neighborhood. He hoped to attract a higher clientele, and he knew a move was necessary.

The Pirates' troubles at Exposition Park coincided with the rapid development of Oakland. Some students at Carnegie Tech who had formed a football team discovered a vacant lot less than two hundred yards away from the Carnegie Library and Schenley Park to use as their home field. The school leased the property from the Commonwealth Real Estate Co. The team cleared large stones and debris from the lot, and played their first game there against the University of Pennsylvania on October 31, 1907[32]. Upon the suggestion of Andrew Carnegie, Barney Dreyfuss attended that game, and immediately thought the site would be worthy of consideration for his new park. After deciding on this lot as his site, Dreyfuss asked Carnegie for some assistance in acquiring the property. As one of the executors of Mrs. Schenley's estate. Carnegie could pressure the city to sell the land, part of the original property sold by Mrs. Schenley to the city in 1889. On October 18, 1908, Dreyfuss purchased the seven-acre property from the Commonwealth Real Estate Co. The property was bordered by Bouquet Street on the west side and Louisa Street on the north.

The purchase agreement was subject to several conditions. Dreyfuss was required by Carnegie to make the ballpark fireproof and harmonious with the other structures in the Schenley Park district[33]. The project would require substantial capital from Dreyfuss, but he believed it to be a worthy investment.

Dreyfuss's next move was to choose someone to design his ballpark. He selected Charles W. Leavitt, Jr., an architect and engineer from New York.

Leavitt had planned and supervised the construction of nearly all of the racetrack stands and clubhouses in the eastern United States, including Belmont Park and

Empire City in Yonkers[34]. Due to the fireproof provision in the contract, the frame for the park had to be made of steel. Carnegie Tech's lease did not expire until December 31, 1908, so construction could not begin until the new year. Dreyfuss tapped Frank Nicola's company to build the park.

Ground was broken at the site on January 2, 1909, a day later than originally planned. A hollow, known as St. Pierre Ravine, ran through the property, so its filling was the first item of business for Nicola's workers. The task required 11,155 tons of dirt and fill. Over 60,000 cubic yards of dirt were graded to make the playing field level. A retaining wall using 2,000 cubic yards of concrete was built to hold the landfill. 35 Night shifts were run by Nicola's men, complete with lights, so that the park could be ready to open early in the season. Although this was a very wet winter, the construction was largely unaffected as the property seemed to be a good one for natural drainage.

By the end of February, the actual construction of the park was set to begin. Dreyfuss's only major stipulation to Leavitt was that the majority of seats in the park be suitable for premium pricing[36]. This idea, a radical one at the time, was consistent with Dreyfuss's firm belief that baseball could become a pleasure for the leisure class. It would also serve as a major source of revenue for Dreyfuss, as profits/ticket would increase substantially. Because Panther Hollow, a one-hundred-yard-wide space that stretched for miles, lay behind the lot and separated it from Schenley Park, the design of the park was largely determined by nature. The rolling hills of the park made it an obvious choice for the backdrop of the new stadium, and the path of the sun directed the placement of the grandstand.

The Nicola Building Company began construction of the grandstand on March 1, 1909, and by March 21, the Raymond Concrete Piling Co. had put in the concrete to support the stands. Double-shifts and good weather allowed the project to proceed rapidly, and by May 9, Dreyfuss announced that the park would open on June 30. Seven acres of sod were brought from Crestline,

Ohio, to complete the playing field, and the project was completed in less than six months.

The grandstand was constructed in four basic units. The first was a large amphitheater of concrete steps, starting eight feet above field level and rising up 28 rows, encompassing 12,500 seats. This was the main section of the park, with ramps connecting it to the street.

The next unit, a balcony, was the same length as the lower unit, suspended on steel columns with cantilevered trusses. The balcony had 12 steep rows, providing 5,500 seats. The front row of the balcony hung over the fifth row of the lower deck. The executive offices of the team were located at the back of the balcony behind home plate, between the first two levels.

The third unit was a series of roof boxes on top of the balcony. These boxes were held by steel supports and were intended to serve the more wealthy customers at the new ballpark. Leavitt insisted that elevators be available to take the fans to and from their roof boxes on the third level from the ground floor. These seats provided a quiet seat away from the expectedly rowdy patrons, complete with a superb view of Schenley Park. An article in the Pittsburgh Press on March 7, 1909, questioned "whether the fans will be able to concentrate on the game," with so many beautiful distractions.

The final unit of the grandstand was used for non-seating purposes.

Eight ticket windows allowed patrons to purchase all grandstand seats at the intersection of Bouquet and Louisa Streets behind home plate. The umpires' room was to the right of the main entrance. Beyond this, the home and visiting clubhouses were equipped with lockers, baths, and dryers for clothes.

The clubhouses were accessible from the field, and a private exit for the players was located underneath the right end of the grandstand.

At the end of the grandstand down the left field foul line, a section of bleachers was completed by March 28. This section was separated from the grandstand only slightly and seated 6,000 in forty-three rows. A garage for automobiles was located under the bleachers, and although it later appeared to be small, it was the city's largest in 1909. Ticket windows for the bleachers were located at the end of the grandstand on Louisa Street, and four thousand square feet of space under the grandstand was kept open for fan protection in case of rain. Temporary bleachers were to be set up deep in the outfield, to be replaced when the ground settled by more permanent seats.

The final section of the ballpark, consisting of three rows of private boxes, was in front of the lower grandstand. These seats were the closest to the field, with the first row being only four feet away. An empty field just beyond the outfield wall was eventually used for Oakland Little League games and became known as Plaza Field.

Dreyfuss arranged seating plans and prices well before the season began. The private boxes at field level contained eight seats and could be obtained for $10/game. These seats were completely sold out by mid-June, and ticket holders had their names engraved on a removable brass plate above their seats. The lower deck of the grandstand was made up of reserved seats, available for $1.00/seat, with the last few rows as general admission for $0.75. A seat in the left field bleachers sold for $0.50, and one in the temporary bleachers could be had for a quarter. Roof boxes, which held seven people, were sold for $8.75/box.

Several other features of the park made it truly revolutionary. Besides the ramps, elevators, and roomy clubhouses, a new canvas infield tarp, to be used during periods of rain, would rise from underneath the field in foul territory behind the third base line and could be rolled over the entire infield in one piece. The space under the grandstand would allow people shelter in case of rain, a feature previously unheard of in Major League parks. The smoke and dust that filled the air at Exposition Park were nowhere to be found at the new park, as the nearest steel mill was not even in sight.

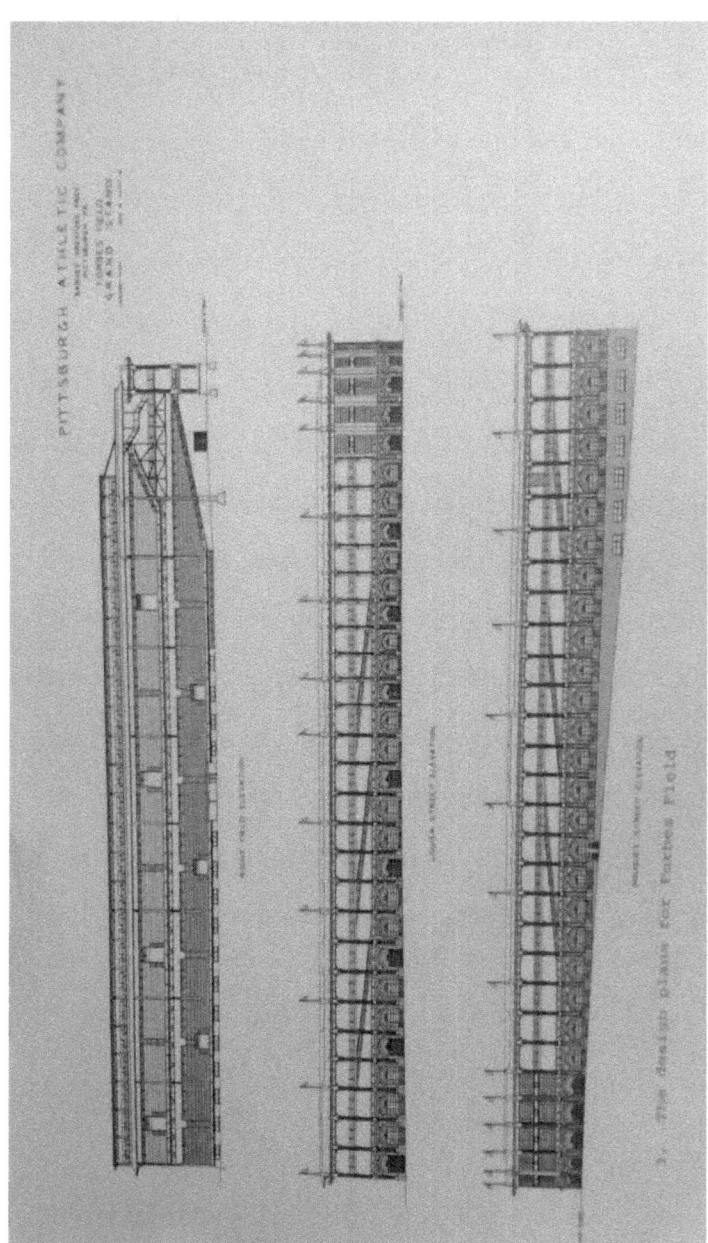

3. The design plans for Forbes Field

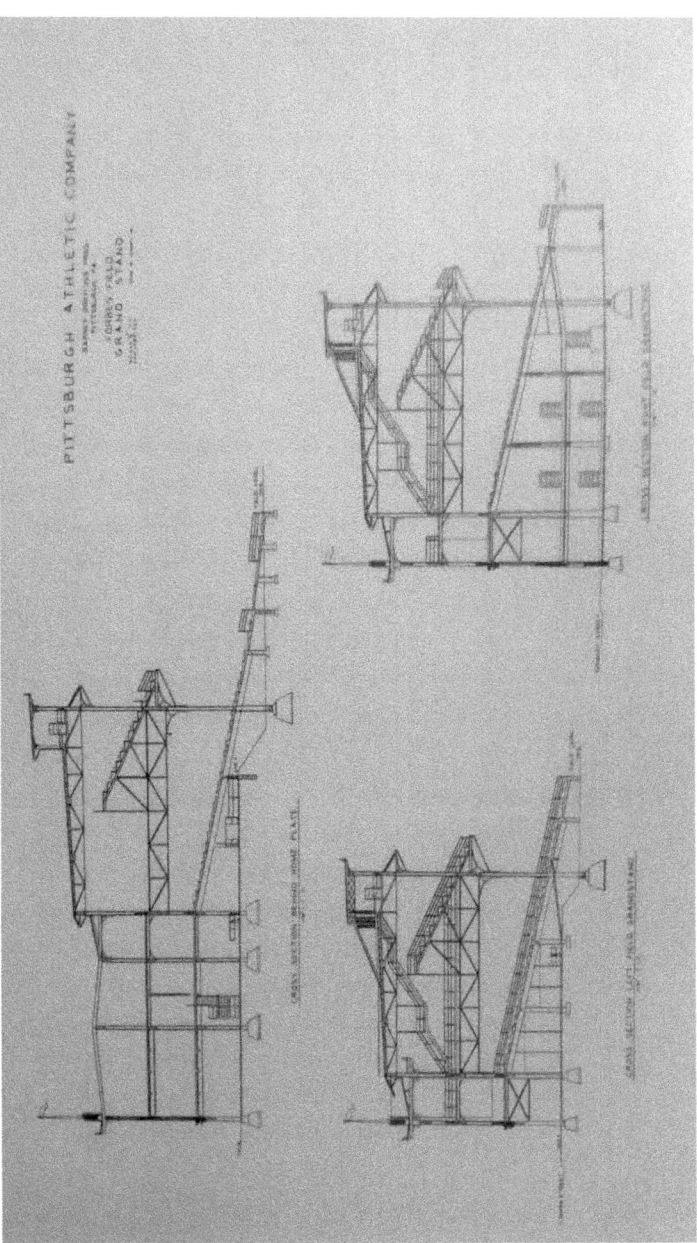

PITTSBURGH ATHLETIC COMPANY

FORBES FIELD
GRAND STAND

The excitement leading up to the opening game at the new ballpark was extreme. First, Dreyfuss would have to come up with a name for the new ballpark. The owner decided that the public should choose the name of the park through a contest. This would provide publicity for the new facility and the team, and the Pittsburgh Press was chosen as the forum. On March 1, 1909, coupons were printed in the paper, and people were asked to submit a name for the park. The fan with the winning entry would receive free admission to every game for the first year. Suggestions included "Dryner Park" for Honus Wagner and Barney Dreyfuss, and "Dreyfuss Park" in honor of the man whose vision produced the park.37 Sometime between March 28 and May 23, Dreyfuss chose the entry of "Forbes Field" as the winner. John Forbes, a hero from the Revolutionary War, had already lent his name to the city's largest street, part of which ran parallel to Louisa Street one block from the new ballpark. Now, the ballpark would also share his name.

Dreyfuss declared the week of June 30 to July 7, 1909, as dedication week for Forbes Field. All railroads leading into Pittsburgh had special rates for that week. The stage was set for opening day.

The sky was without a cloud on June 30, 1909, a beautiful day in Pittsburgh. The game, pitting the Pirates against the Chicago Cubs, was scheduled to begin at 2:30 pm. However, fans began to arrive at the park by 9:00, waiting in line for General Admission and Bleacher tickets. By the time the ticket windows opened at 10:00 am, Bouquet and Louisa streets were filled with fans. The gates opened at noon, and a mad rush of more than 5,000 fans clamored for the unreserved seats. Soon, the crowd in the temporary bleachers became so filled with standing room patrons that the outfield section was roped off. At 1:30 pm., dedication ceremonies began with two processions, each led by a band down the respective foul lines. The bands met at home plate, proceeding to march to the center field flag pole, where the American flag was raised, eliciting a roar from the crowd. By game time, 30,338 people had entered the park.

Mayor Christopher Magee threw out the first ball at the game. Other dignitaries in the audience included National League President Harry Pulliam (Dreyfuss's former employee and friend), American League President Ban Johnson, Congressman John Tener, and Eddie Morris, a member of Pittsburgh's 1885 Union Association team. Bob Emslie and Hank O'Day were introduced as the umpires for the game, and the Pirates took the Field.

The Cubs scored a run in the first inning after Johnny Evers, the first batter, was hit by a pitch from Pirate pitcher Vic Willis. Evers scored on a Frank Chance single to center field. The score remained 1-0 Cubs until the bottom of the sixth, when Dots Miller followed Honus Wagner's single with his own to push the shortstop across home plate and even the score. Chicago scored twice in the top of the eighth, and the Pirates rallied to score a run in the bottom half of the inning. Manager Fred Clarke felt the team should have been awarded another run due to an errant ruling on Dots Miller's drive to center field. The ball rolled into the crowd, and first baseman Bill Abstein crossed the plate, but was returned to third base by the umpires as the hit was declared a ground rule double. The Pirates could not muster any more runs off the stingy Cub pitching staff, and the team's debut at Forbes Field was spoiled.

However, the outcome of the game could not spoil the grandeur of the new ballpark. Baseball Magazine exclaimed, "The new park is the greatest achievement in civil engineering and as beautiful as well as secure a construction as has been undertaken in this country[38]." Another publication raved about the park and its opening.

"The formal opening of Forbes Field was an historic event; the full significance could be better felt than expressed. Words must fail to picture to the mind's eye adequately the splendor of the magnificent pile President Dreyfuss erected as a tribute to the National game, a beneficence to Pittsburgh, and an enduring monument to himself. For architectural beauty, imposing size, solid construction, public comfort and convenience, it has not its superior in the world[39]."

Fortunately for Dreyfuss, the final score at Forbes Field's opener was not indicative of the team's success that season. In fact, Fred Clarke, caught up in the magic that filled the air that final day in June 1909, said after the game, "We will win the World Series this season[40]." Clarke's prophecy followed the team throughout the summer, as Wagner led the league in batting again with a .339 average and 100 RBIs. Willis won 22 games, Howie Caminitz 25, Lefty Leifield 19, Nick Maddox 13, and rookie Babe Adams 12. In total, the team won 110 games in 1909 and met the Detroit Tigers, led by Ty Cobb, in the World Series[41].

Young Adams was the Pirates' savior, winning games 1 and 5, and solidifying the staff despite poor performances by Willis, Caminitz, and Leifield. The series was even after six games, and the Pirates travelled to Detroit for the seventh and deciding game. Adams pitched again, this time shutting the Tigers out and bringing the championship title back to Pittsburgh. Wagner outshone Cobb in their personal duel, hitting better than the Georgia Peach, and provided many false stories about Cobb and the Series in later years.

The World Series games played at Forbes Field that fall were just as exciting as the opening game in June. The three games at Forbes Field attracted 82,885 fans. 42 In fact, the entire season was a pleasant dream for Dreyfuss, who had vaulted himself, his team, and his park into the national spotlight. Years later, Dreyfuss liked to tell stories of people laughing at him for building a park "where there was nothing but a few cows and a hothouse." The reality of the matter is that there was quite a bit of activity going on around the site where he would erect Forbes Field, and Barney Dreyfuss probably reasoned that there would soon be more. Although he wanted people to think of him as a genius for building Forbes Field in Oakland, Dreyfuss' actions were nothing more than sensible.

A new era had descended upon baseball, as ten new steel parks were built over the next five years. More importantly, though, Forbes Field added a new dimension to Oakland, the city's emerging cultural center. Not only would the area be home to concerts, poetry readings, fine homes, theater performances, and a lavish hotel, but now baseball and other entertainment functions would call Oakland home. The construction of Forbes Field would change Oakland and Pittsburgh forever.

CHAPTER 4: A PLACE FOR ALL PEOPLE

The years immediately following the construction of Forbes Field saw the continued expansion of Franklin Nicola's monumental quarter in Oakland. The Allegheny County Soldiers and Sailors War Memorial was completed in 1911. It included an auditorium for 2,500, a memorial, meeting rooms, and a banquet hall for the remaining Civil War veterans[43]. The building was situated on the hill, 50 yards from the corner of Bigelow Boulevard and Fifth Avenue, with the space in front of it left open to maintain a clear vista. Both the Memorial's design and its vast grounds were clearly connected to Nicola's vision for Oakland.

Still, the social section of Frank Nicola's plan was incomplete. However, by 1915, many clubhouses were erected along Fifth Avenue and up the hill from it. The first and most eloquent of these was the Pittsburgh Athletic Association, commonly referred to as the P.A.A.

This building, located at the corner of Fifth Avenue and Lytton Street, was completed by 1911 and served as a gathering place for gentlemen who engaged in the sporting life. The P.A.A. was one block east of Soldiers and Sailors on Fifth Avenue, and handsomely complemented the Memorial.

The Masonic Temple, a meeting and gathering facility for the thousands of masons across the Pittsburgh area, was built directly across Lytton Street from the P.A.A. on Fifth Avenue in 1914. It was followed in 1915 by the Syria Mosque, a distinctive yet unique building located on Bigelow Boulevard, just around the corner from the War Memorial. The mosque was built as a religious shrine, but is more widely known as the home of the Pittsburgh Symphony and Opera, featuring a 3,700-seat concert hall.

Several other social clubs were erected within Nicola's 105-acre plot. The Twentieth Century Club was built across from the Memorial on Bigelow Boulevard in 1910 as an upper-crust gathering place for Protestants, and was followed by its next-door neighbor, the

Historical Society of Western Pennsylvania, in 1912. The Concordia Club was built one block west of Bigelow Boulevard (then known as O'Hara Street) and served the Jewish elite of the entire city.

The construction of these buildings truly promoted Oakland as the civic center of Pittsburgh. Not only were people encouraged to move to Oakland by these attractions, but most were drawn there for a majority of their activities. Virtually all forms of culture and entertainment were found in Oakland. However, the educational quarter of Oakland was still in its early stages of development.

The University of Pittsburgh, which purchased land in Oakland earlier, actually moved from Observatory Hill on the North Side of the city to Oakland just before Forbes Field opened its turnstiles in the summer of 1909[44]. Henry Hornbostel had designed, and Nicola had constructed four buildings that were to serve as the cornerstone of the "Acropolis" plan for the University campus. The first brick of the Mineral Industries Building (later known as State Hall) was laid the same day in 1908 as the first brick for the War Memorial. Nine months later, Thaw Hall was built on O'Hara Street as the University's engineering building. The medical school, to be known as Pennsylvania Hall, was built above these buildings on the hill. By 1912, a fourth building (Allen Hall) was added as part of the Acropolis plan.

The Acropolis plan and other University activities were interrupted by American involvement in World War I. In April 1918, the federal government established barracks and classes to train auto and gas engine mechanics at the University. This attracted thousands of military trainees, and a medical training facility was set up on the campus to train surgeons, nurses, and orderlies[45]. By September of that same year, Pitt and 524 other colleges were "taken over" by the federal government to train student officers for the war. This, coupled with a 40-day quarantine that resulted from a major influenza epidemic, slowed any construction efforts at the University. Still, by the war's end, the University campus was more congested than ever.

Chancellor Samuel McCormick wanted to continue to expand with Hornbostel's disrupted Acropolis plan. However, this plan became very expensive, as the costs of the four previously erected buildings largely exceeded their projections. In 1920, Chancellor McCormick chose to abandon the Hornbostel plan and adopt the more modest designs of Benno Janssen, who had entered the original contest to design Pitt's campus in 1908. Janssen's plan was dependent upon McCormick's support, though, and the Chancellor was ready to retire.

The new chancellor, Dr. John Bowman, decided to abandon the "hill campus" completely for a building that "will tell of the spirit of Pittsburgh[46]." Bowman conceived of a great tower, a high-rise building, to house most of the University's classrooms, laboratories, social activities, libraries, and various schools. Bowman set out to raise money for the building, but people were hesitant to make donations to a project that was so outrageous and still in its infancy.

Dr. Bowman decided to find a site for his high building as he continued to solicit money for its construction. His first choice was the rectangular plot that lay between Fifth and Forbes Avenues, across the street (on the Southwest corner) from the beautiful Schenley Hotel. This area, known as Frick Acres, was home to several mansions, gardens, tennis courts, and open fields. It was also (at the North) across from the fairly new clubhouses and other monumental structures in Oakland along Fifth Avenue. Bowman tried to obtain this lot, but the Frick Trustees were asking for $1.5 million. The University did not have the money, and Bowman knew very few sources in Pittsburgh who did. Richard B. Mellon, the wealthy vice president of Mellon National Bank, was a Pitt trustee and Bowman's initial supporter in the project. He told Bowman that the Chancellor must convince his older brother and bank president, A.W. Mellon, to buy the Frick Acres for Pitt. After months of persistence and explanations of necessity by Bowman, A.W. Mellon agreed to buy the land for the University, and even paid all of Pitt's previous debts so that Bowman could begin the project with a clean slate[47].

The chancellor, along with his assistant, John Weber, and architect Charles Klauder, estimated the construction costs at $10 million. After much debate among the trustees concerning the costs and design, work began on clearing Frick Acres for the construction of the Cathedral of Learning, a tall building. By May 8, 1928, the steel skeleton of the Cathedral was beginning to go up. The frame was completed by 1930, but further construction was halted because of financial difficulties[48]. Funds had been depleted, and the Great Depression, which had occurred two years earlier, had a crushing effect on donations to the building fund. Franklin Roosevelt's New Deal aided the Cathedral greatly through the Civil Works Administration. The CWA alloted a large grant to the University, and by 1937, the Cathedral was 90 percent complete.

The Cathedral, all forty-two stories of its Gothic grandeur, was unlike any college building in the nation. A tall building was built just before the Cathedral at the University of Nebraska, but it was not nearly as grandiose. In fact, the Cathedral of Learning was the nation's second-tallest building at the time of its completion (the Woolworth Building in Manhattan was the first). After A.W. Mellon agreed to finance the $500,000 necessary to complete the project, the cornerstone was laid for the Commons Room (in the lobby) on June 4, 1937[49]. The Cathedral was now home to the library, the law school, most classrooms, the faculty club, student facilities, and University offices.

Soon after, Bowman's Nationality Rooms would be built inside the Cathedral as a tribute to the many nations from which Pitt students hailed. By 1938, two more Gothic buildings, Heinz Chapel and the Stephen Foster Memorial, were built on the Cathedral lawn. The University of Pittsburgh was no longer known as a school on a hill. Although some of the campus still remained above Fifth Avenue, the construction of the great Cathedral and its accompanying buildings drew the focus of University administrators and the public to it. No longer was the center of the campus to rise above the rest of Oakland from atop the hill over Schenley Farms;

rather, Pitt would tower above Pittsburgh from below the hill, expanding further south into Oakland.

Although the conception and construction of the Cathedral of Learning occupied a great deal of energy, time, and money, it was not the University's only significant expansion project in the 1920s and 1930s. Actually, two other meaningful projects began before the Cathedral.

One was the building of a football stadium on the hillside of the upper campus. Collegiate football had become extremely popular in the area, and Coach Glenn "Pop" Warner's Pitt teams won national recognition by 1918[50]. Strong support from the 11,000 alumni and 9,000 students, each entitled to two seats, meant that the 25,000 seats available at Forbes Field, which Dreyfuss had rented to Pitt for sixteen years, were no longer adequate. Bowman purchased a nine-acre estate at the northwest edge of the hill campus on DeSoto Street in 1923. Ground was broken for the stadium on August 7, 1924, and the work was completed slightly more than one year later on September 1, 1925[51]. The stadium was primarily used for football games and seated 65,000. It provided yet another attraction in the Oakland area.

The other major project of the Bowman administration was the building of the medical center. Despite its dense population, no large medical complex like the Mayo Clinic existed in Western Pennsylvania. Dr. Bowman and Dr. Huggins, the Dean of the School of Medicine, recognized the need for great hospitals to which the University could ally itself, as well as the city's need for a medical center. These two needs could be combined, they felt, in Oakland. The first hospital to join the medical center was the Elizabeth Steel Magee Hospital for Women, named after the mother of former Mayor Christopher Magee. The hospital, located at the southern intersection of Forbes Avenue and Halket Street, naturally took over the University's gynecology department by 1921. Bowman recognized the need for more hospitals in the medical center and wanted to create a "complex" for them. He was able to make this happen when he purchased the 12-acre Porter estate just west of Schenley Farms on the hillside. There, Children's

Hospital, which became tied to the University in 1922, erected a building in 1926[52]. By 1930, construction had begun on The Presbyterian Hospital and its neighbor, The Eye and Ear Hospital. The Falk Clinic, opened in 1931, was to serve as a permanent outpatient dispensary for the medical school. The School of Dentistry was also added along the hillside in 1928. Thus, the medical center was in full force even before the Cathedral of Learning, and came to dominate the University's upper campus with its hospitals and research facilities.

By the end of the 1930s, the University of Pittsburgh was, in many ways, the dominant force in the city of Pittsburgh. It was the center of education, medicine, and athletics (football) for its students, alumni, faculty, staff, and other Western Pennsylvanians. All of these activities occurred on campus, directly in the Oakland area that had been so desolate at the turn of the century.

Still, Frank Nicola's quarters and the University of Pittsburgh were not the only developing areas in Oakland. South of the Cathedral of Learning and Forbes Avenue, another section of Oakland was being fashioned closer to Forbes Field. Before the baseball monument was built, a small wave of Italian immigrants swept into the cliff behind Bates Street, which was known as Panther Hollow, a large expanse of space that separated parts of South Oakland from Schenley Park. Just one block south of the ballpark along Bouquet Street, Gaetano Diulius moved his family to the Hollow in the 1890s as he looked for work[53]. The area, located just beneath Schenley Park, offered a beautiful and serene setting for homes without the high costs of land and construction. Several other Italian families followed Diulius into the Hollow and at the edge of the cliff in South Oakland. Soon, the cross streets below Forbes Avenue were filled with Irish and Italian Catholics. Some opened barber shops, restaurants, and small grocery stores there, while others worked in Schenley Park. Churches were built, mostly Catholic, although a number of Greek and Syrian Orthodox shrines were established there[54]. Clearly, a strong ethnic working-class community existed in Oakland, and it grew with the construction of Forbes Field.

Above the hollow, many other entrepreneurs followed Frank Nicola's Schenley Hotel on Forbes Street with buildings of their own. The Iriquois Apartments were built on the opposite side of Forbes Street from the hotel, just four blocks west. The Flannery Building, a complex of shops and apartments, was built across from the Iriquois in 1911. Many more homes were erected south of Forbes Street, just above the Hollow on Dawson, Bates, and Semple streets, with an architectural flavor of Naples, Italy.

Schenley Park was also beginning to draw a larger working-class constituency, as was its original purpose. For its first thirty years, the park was the domain of the wealthy, but with the establishment of the new residential district in South Oakland, Schenley Park became more accessible to the general public.

More recreational facilities, such as an ice skating rink and a swimming pool, were signs of the park's transformation.

Thus, two very different sections of Oakland had developed by the end of the 1930s. North of Forbes Avenue was Frank Nicola's Oakland, complete with monuments, clubhouses, fine homes, and the University of Pittsburgh's classrooms, its medical center, and it's stadium. South of Forbes was an evolving immigrant neighborhood, crowded with small homes and stores. Forbes Field was also situated in the midst of this neighborhood and would become an important part of that community. The Carnegie Institute and Schenley Park, despite their location south of Forbes, were more clearly connected to Nicola's Oakland through their beauty and cultural functions. And, in the middle of these two vastly different, though very congenial parts of Oakland was the Cathedral of Learning. Its location signaled Pitt's readiness to expand into South Oakland, and was the first sign of trouble for Forbes Field.

CHAPTER 5: TRIUMPH, TRAGEDY, TECHNOLOGY

The growth and development of Oakland in the first half of the twentieth century did not consist only of Pitt's expansion and Nicola's grand buildings. Rather, Forbes Field attracted another type of individual to Oakland and its confines, the baseball fan. Although it would be 16 years until the Pirates repeated their World Series performance of 1909, baseball at Forbes Field was still a happening. The ballpark brought outsiders to South Oakland and became a fixture in the lives of those who already lived there.

The 1910 season was a major setback for the Pirates, as the Bucs finished in third place following their World Series victory. Barney Dreyfuss put it best when he said, "Our 1910 team was my biggest disappointment in baseball. Never did I see a great team fold so quickly[55]." Indeed, the club's golden pitching arms went sour after 1909, as did the desire for fans to attend games.

Attendance at Forbes Field dropped to 296,000 by 1913, despite the fact that the club remained in the first division. The fans, initially overwhelmed by the mere presence of Forbes Field, were now attending games based on the team's talent level. Although Honus Wagner continued to dazzle all with his abilities and newcomer Max Carey raced around the base paths with extraordinary speed, the team could not win consistently. The tough times culminated in the parting of ways between Dreyfuss and Fred Clarke after the 1915 season. In 1914, the Pirates finished in seventh place and drew only 139,620. The next season, the club remained in the second division, finishing only slightly higher (in fifth place). Clarke, who had managed and played for Dreyfuss in Louisville since 1897, was the scapegoat for the team's poor finishes.

Dreyfuss soon realized that Clarke's stubborn nature was not the only reason for the team's lackluster performances. Errant personnel moves by Dreyfuss himself, such as the one that allowed George Sisler, a young first baseman who would go on to the Hall of

Fame, to become a member of the St. Louis Browns, hurt team chemistry. The fiery Jimmy Callahan was hired to replace Clarke in 1916, but fared no better than his predecessor. Another second division finish, this time in sixth place, and a 20-40 start in 1917 prompted Dreyfuss to fire Callahan. In an attempt to boost interest in the team, Dreyfuss persuaded Wagner, now only a .265 hitter and part-time player, to manage the club. This experiment lasted only five games, though, as Wagner quit and was replaced by Hugo Bedzek. Dreyfuss was highly ridiculed in the press, and only 192,807 fans came to Forbes Field that summer. For the first time under Dreyfuss, the Pirates finished in last place for the 1917 season. Honus Wagner retired that fall, ending a career that many feel was the greatest of anyone who ever played the game of baseball. His career statistics of 1,732 RBI's, eight batting titles, 722 stolen bases, 17 seasons hitting over .300, and a daunting presence at shortstop made him an easy selection for enshrinement in the Baseball Hall of Fame[56]. Honus Wagner's retirement marked the end of an era in Pirate baseball, the latter part of which Barney Dreyfuss would rather have forgotten by 1917.

Baseball in Pittsburgh and throughout the nation was affected by World War I. For the first time ever, Dreyfuss allowed an advertisement to be placed on the outfield wall of Forbes Field. No one worried that Dreyfuss was losing his integrity, though, as the sign was for patriotic purposes, asking people to buy U.S. war bonds. Many Pirates served in the military as the team compiled three consecutive fourth-place finishes from 1918 to 1920. Dreyfuss, who still scouted for players himself, improved the team greatly by signing a young shortstop in Massachusetts named Harold "Pie" Traynor. He appeared in 17 games in 1920 and was moved to third base when Dreyfuss traded for Rabbit Maranville, a veteran shortstop. These two players, combined with the outfield combination of the now seasoned Max Carey and young Carson Bigbee, proved to be a formidable group. Despite the team's improvement that season under Manager George Gibson, the catcher on the 1909 club, the Pirates finished second to John McGraw's New York Giants.

The 1921 season was pivotal for the Pirates, as it reestablished their presence both within the league and in the Oakland community. Attendance at Forbes Field skyrocketed to a then-record 701,567. Children who lived in Oakland also became very attached to the ballpark and the team. During the summer, it was a common sight for youngsters to wait by the players' entrance on Bouquet Street. Sometimes, the children were even allowed to accompany their favorite Pirate into the clubhouse and be sent free to roam the stands or run errands. Art McKennan, who lived a few blocks from Forbes Field on Dawson Street, was a teenager when first baseman Billy Southworth introduced him to the clubhouse man at the ballpark, who often sent McKennan to get a pie and a bottle of milk for each player's lunch[57]. This type of relationship between young fans and players would create a strong bond and an even stronger fan base. Many star players began to live in the neighborhood around the ballpark. Pie Traynor roomed in a house on

Fifth Avenue, and Rabbit Maranville lived on Dawson Street[58]. Forbes Street and its intersections at Atwood, Meyran, and Oakland Avenues became sights where fans could spot their favorite players eating a meal, having a drink, or taking a walk. There was little need to leave Oakland, for everything the players needed was within walking distance. Thus, although not every Pirate called Oakland home, the neighborhood around Forbes Field became very important to the team.

The Bucs finished third for the next three seasons as Bill McKechnie was hired to replace Gibson, who inexplicably left the team. Kiki Cuyler joined the team as an outfielder in 1923, and Glenn Wright as shortstop in 1924, moving Rabbit Maranville to second base. The stage was set for triumph in 1925.

Before that season began, Dreyfuss was eager to win the pennant. To accomplish this goal, he felt it necessary to make changes to his roster. His biggest move came when he traded Maranville, pitcher Wilbur Cooper, and first baseman Charlie Grimm to the Chicago Cubs. Maranville and Grimm were known to be good-time fellows, displaying conduct that Dreyfuss felt was detrimental to the team[59]. The owner also saw Cooper's career fading and wanted to get some young talent for him. The trade changed the team's attitude and helped the Pirates capture their first NL Pennant since 1909. The play of Kiki Cuyler and Max Carey didn't hurt either, as both had career years at the plate. Traynor was his consistent self, batting .320 and driving in 120 runs, and second baseman Eddie Moore drew a league-high 73 walks while leading off in the batting order[60]. The season was also highlighted by the return of Fred Clarke to the dugout. Clark, who was still a stockholder in the club, was brought back by Dreyfuss to assist McKechnie as a coach[61].

Dreyfuss also made another major change to Pittsburgh baseball before the 1925 season. Attendance at Forbes Field had jumped to a new high of 736,833 in 1924, and the owner felt more seats should be available. Thus, double-decked stands were added in right field, with 7,000 more seats made available. Forbes Field now had 32,000 permanent seats, with room for more with temporary bleachers and standing room.

The Pirates' opponents in the 1925 World Series were the Washington Senators, led by thirty-seven-year-old pitching ace Walter Johnson. The first game of the best-of-seven series was held at Forbes Field. Barney Dreyfuss had long awaited the return of the Series to Pittsburgh, and he provided much pomp and circumstance for the opening game. 41,723 fans packed into Forbes Field to see the heroes from the 1909 World Series, Honus Wagner and Ty Cobb, introduced to the crowd. Wooden bleachers were inserted along the outfield wall to provide additional seats[62]. Kiki Cuyler was presented with a gold bat and ball, and the game was set to begin.

Walter Johnson stifled the Pirate offensive attack as the Senators won the first game easily, 4-1. The great Christy Mathewson passed away before Game 2, so the flag at Forbes Field flew at half-mast, and players from both squads wore armbands[63]. Washington shortstop Roger Peckinpaugh's error helped the Bucs win 3-2, and even the series at one game each.

The series moved back to Washington for Game 3, and didn't disappoint.

The game featured Washington centerfielder Sam Rice diving into the temporary bleachers for a fly ball and emerging from the crowd several seconds later with the ball in hand. Umpire Charley Rigler called the Pirate batter out, and the Bucs lost the game. Immediately afterwards, Dreyfuss protested the game to Judge Kennesaw Mountain Landis, the Commissioner of Baseball, who rejected the protest. The Senators had the lead in the series, two games to one[64].

In the fourth game, Walter Johnson blanked the Pirates, this time allowing six hits and no runs, as the Pirates went quietly. The Senators now held a three games to one lead, a deficit from which no team in World Series history had come back to win the championship.

The Bucs scraped out a 6-3 victory in Game Five to send the Series back to Forbes Field for Game Six. Another crucial error by Roger Peckinpaugh in the third inning helped the Pirates, and a home run by Eddie Moore finished the Senators, 3-2. The series would come down to one final game, and it would be a memorable one.

Walter Johnson was slated to start for Washington, but the game was delayed by rain. Many fans who attended the game felt it should not have been played, but the umpires allowed the game to begin. Washington scored four runs in the first inning, surely more than enough protection for the crafty "Big Train". The game was filled with fielding blunders (Peckinpaugh made yet another crucial error to keep a Pirate rally alive in the 8th inning), and a grand slam in the 8th for Cuyler that was called a ground rule double because the umpires couldn't see the ball. The Bucs went on to win the game 9-7, and thus the World Series, but the game should probably have been postponed and played the following day.

The 1925 World Series was also a highlight for many young men in Oakland. Some were given a chance to work at Forbes Field by Gus Miller, the head usher at the ballpark for many years. Miller, who owned a newsstand at the corner of Forbes and Bouquet Streets since 1909, knew many families in the area well and recruited young men to work games for him at Forbes Field. This was an enticing offer, as it allowed them to watch Pirate games for free, so Miller did not have to beg. Rather, he demanded that anyone wishing to usher for him buy their cigarettes or chewing tobacco at his newsstand, if they indulged in those habits[65]. Miller was also notorious for his confusing messages to his ushers, such as, "Ok now, double-up in single file and follow me," and "You two form a circle. [66]" Although Miller's antics were often the source of laughter, his effect on the youth of Oakland was undeniable. Gus Miller was yet another element in the growing attachment between the people of Oakland and Forbes Field.

The 1926 season, which followed the World Series, was not as successful for the Pirates. Although the team finished a respectable third, drew well, and introduced a young rookie named Paul Waner to the rest of the league, the season was marred by internal strife. Fred Clarke, still serving the team as an assistant to Bill McKechnie, suggested to him that Max Carey, who was thirty-six years old, be benched. Carson Bigbee overheard the conversation, told Babe Adams about it, and Adams said, "Only the manager should manage," in effect telling Clarke to mind his own business[67]. When Carey got word of the incident, he asked the players to vote Clarke out of the dugout. They did not, and Clarke soon heard about this "scandal" himself. He demanded that the players responsible be punished, and Barney Dreyfuss acted accordingly. Before the 1926 season was over, Bigbee, Adams, and Carey were no longer Pirates. McKechnie was also fired after the season. The entire episode, later known as the Fred Clarke Mutiny, served as an example that Barney Dreyfuss would not tolerate disunity and was still in control of his team.

Despite the difficulties of the 1926 club, the Pirates remained a talented bunch and were poised to repeat their performance of two seasons earlier. Dreyfuss hired Donnie Bush to manage the team before the 1927 season. The addition of Lloyd Waner, the younger brother of Paul, provided the Bucs with an even more potent attack. Lloyd, nicknamed Little Poison, quickly became recognized for his prowess in centerfield. Together with Cuyler, they provided the punch to move the Pirates past the New York Giants and St. Louis Browns and into the World Series.

Their opponents in that series were the mighty New York Yankees, led by the Murderer's Row tandem of Babe Ruth and Lou Gehrig. Despite strong hitting by the Bucs, they were no match for the powerful Yankees, who swept them in four games. Although fans were disappointed with the series' result, most were awed by the Yankees' presence. Oaklanders, in particular, were treated to views of Babe Ruth smoking cigars on the porch at the Schenley Hotel. Some other residents were lucky enough to meet the Bambino. Thus, despite the loss, the 1927 World Series helped to heighten fan interest in baseball and drew the people of Oakland even closer to their ballpark.

Barney Dreyfuss dismantled the club after the 1927 season by trading away Kiki Cuyler to Chicago for two disappointing young prospects. Again, Dreyfuss' decision was fueled by a player's detrimental conduct, as Cuyler had refused to be moved up in the batting order earlier in the season. Dreyfuss did not forget about Cuyler's antics, and he destroyed what may have become the greatest outfield of all time with the trade.

The team was mired in mediocrity for the next few seasons, despite the consistently strong play of the Waner brothers. A fourth-place finish in 1928, a second-place finish in 1929 (although they were 10.5 games behind the leader), and two fifth-place finishes in 1930 & 1931 convinced fans to stay away from Forbes Field. In fact, by 1931, attendance fell to 260,392. This trouble at the box office, though, would not be as damaging as the trouble in the team's front office.

Tragedy struck the Pirate organization on February 19, 1931, as Sammy Dreyfuss, son of Barney, and vice president, treasurer, and business manager of the team, died of pneumonia at the age of thirty-six. Barney Dreyfuss was devastated by his son's passing and knew he needed to find a new successor to his position. He was forced to turn to his son-in-law, Bill Benswanger, who was married to his daughter Eleanor. Benswanger was a fan of baseball, but the focus of his life was clearly away from the game. He was in the insurance business, a member of the Pittsburgh Symphony's board, and loved classical music. Despite the clear mismatch between the game and the man, Benswanger heeded his father-in-law's request and came to work for him immediately.

Bill Benswanger arrived on the scene no sooner than Dreyfuss himself would leave it. Barney underwent surgery in New York in January 1932 for a gland problem in his neck, but complications arose. On February 5, 1932, nearly one year after his son died, Barney Dreyfuss passed away. The man who brought credibility to Pittsburgh baseball, who gave Forbes Field to the city and to the entire nation as a monument, and who founded the World Series, was dead. Barney Dreyfuss also served as the National League Schedule Committee chairman for many years and was extremely influential in league matters. NL President John Heydler hailed Dreyfuss as "the esteemed senior baseball man in the country," and went on to exclaim, "He discovered more great players than any other man in the game."

The wife of Barney Dreyfuss took over as chairman of the team immediately, and Bill Benswanger acted as president. The 1932 campaign was a successful one for the Bucs, as George Gibson, rehired by Dreyfuss just before his death, led them to a second-place finish. Arky Vaughan took over at shortstop that season and hit .318. Despite the good fortunes of the Pirates on the diamond, the effects of the Great Depression kept fans away from Forbes Field.

Honus Wagner returned to the team in 1933, seeking employment after suffering financially since his retirement. Benswanger accommodated the former star, hiring him as a coach, a role he would hold for twenty years. His presence, however, was not enough to vault the club into the top spot, as they came in second place again. Benswanger, like Dreyfuss before him, would not tolerate anything less than a pennant, so Gibson was fired. Pie Traynor, the great third baseman, was dubbed the new skipper. Traynor was a lovable and respected man, but could not bring a pennant back to Pittsburgh. His first four teams (1934-37) struggled, but attendance rose to nearly 500,000 by 1937. The advent of Sunday baseball in Pittsburgh enhanced this figure. Pennsylvania's Blue Laws did not allow it, but when they were repealed, Benswanger immediately instituted Sunday games. Just as they had been for Dreyfuss over 40 years earlier in Louisville, Sunday contests regularly drew the largest crowds at Forbes Field.

Boxing became a popular event at Forbes Field in the 1930s. Jersey Joe Walcott won the title there in 1936, and Billy Conn, Pittsburgh's hometown hero, defeated many challengers at the ballpark. Other activities at the ballpark included Jehovah's Witness conventions, the Catholic Eucharistic Congress, the circus, and political rallies. The Homestead Grays, a great Negro League team in Pittsburgh, played some of their home games at the ballpark. Although these other attractions gave Dreyfuss and then Benswanger another source of revenue, the most important tenant of Forbes Field was the Pittsburgh Pirates.

Babe Ruth hit his final three home runs at Forbes Field on May 25, 1935, the last of which sailed over the right field roof and into Panther Hollow, making him the first person ever to hit a ball that far. Ruth's appearance drew the most excitement at Forbes Field in years, but Traynor's 1938 club would soon captivate the fans of Pittsburgh.

The Pirates went on a tear in mid-summer and looked as if they would be hosting more World Series games. Benswanger was very optimistic that the World Series was coming back to Forbes Field, and ordered the construction of a fourth deck above home plate to house reporters for the event. The section, known as the Crow's Nest, had a capacity of 600. However, the team finished their home season with a one-and-a-half-game lead on Chicago and a three-game series at Wrigley Field to determine the National League Pennant. The Bucs were swept by the Cubs, as Gabby Hartnett's home run off of Mace Brown in the ninth inning of the second game gave the Cubs the lead in the standings. The Crow's Nest became known as Mace Brown's folly, and the Pirates would encounter many poor seasons in their immediate future.

Mace Brown's folly and the Crow's Nest blunder of 1938 were devastating to the Pittsburgh Pirates, as Bill Benswanger was denied his first trip to the World Series as the chief of the Pirates. Buc fans were also crushed by the loss that season, as only 376,734 came to Forbes Field to watch the team slide to sixth place the following year. Benswanger dismissed the legendary Pie Traynor as manager and replaced him with Frankie Frisch, but to no avail. The Pirates could not recover psychologically from the 1938 season, and the Pittsburgh baseball scene was clearly in need of excitement.

Much of this excitement was provided by way of the transistor. In 1921, the first radio broadcast of a baseball game occurred at Forbes Field. Harold Arlin called the game over on KDKA radio in Pittsburgh, and a new era was born.

In the 1930s, Cincinnati club president Larry MacPhail recognized the potential for expanding the fan base that radio would create and began to have all of his team's games broadcast over the radio. When Bill Benswanger and the executives of KDKA made the decision to follow suit in 1936, the only logical choice for an announcer was the greatest Pirate fan of all. Albert Kennedy "Rosey" Roswell, who could often be seen at Forbes Field as a spectator, helped to introduce baseball and the team he loved to thousands of men, women, and children across the region. Baseball was his religion, and "the Buccos his good book.[68]" Rosey Roswell arrived just in time to rescue the Pirates from despair, and provided the cure for what ailed Pittsburgh baseball.

Rosey pioneered what later became known as the "Midwestern Cheering School," where a team's announcer would root for his team, remaining biased and unobjective throughout the broadcast[69]. Pittsburghers immediately fell in love with Roswell's rooting antics. His descriptions of the action on the field, along with his colorful sayings, allowed Pirates fans to envision the action inside Forbes Field, and eventually other ballparks for away games. Despite the club's lackluster play, Roswell's style kept fans coming to the ballpark. His imagination produced such sayings as "doozie marooney" (a Pirate extra-base hit), "the dipsey doodle" (strikeout by a Pirate pitcher), "oh, my aching back" (after a Pirate loss), and "put on the lamb chops, honey, I'll be home soon" (a Pirate victory) [70]. Perhaps most memorable, though, was Rosey Roswell's home run call. As the baseball hit by a Pirate cleared the wall at Forbes Field, Roswell would exclaim, "Get upstairs, Aunt Minnie, and raise the window! Here she comes!" Immediately following this exclamation, Roswell would signal for one of his assistants to shatter a pane of glass, signifying Aunt Minnie's window breaking. Then Roswell would exclaim, "That's too bad. She tripped over a garden hose! Aunt Minnie never made it!"

This home run call, still the most recognizable of all time, and Rosey's other sayings charmed listeners at home. Roswell used his antics, which later became known as a "Rosey Ramble," to entertain the fans at home, keeping their interest level high despite the Pirates' frequent behind-the-game leads. Women, who were previously a minor part of the Pirates' following, became attracted to the game through Roswell. In fact, many women would not serve dinner until Rosey signed off. He truly entertained Pirate fans at a time when they needed it most.

However, Rosey Roswell, with all of his wit and creativity, could not keep the Pirates afloat by himself. The advent of night baseball complemented Roswell's incessant rooting. In January 1940, Benswanger, again following MacPhail's lead, decided to install lights at Forbes Field so that some games could be played in the evening. A survey taken of the six major league clubs that had lights showed that the average night game attendance was more than five times the average daytime attendance during the 1939 season[71]. Benswanger could not ignore these numbers, and by June, the lights were installed in eight steel towers. The first night game at Forbes Field was played on June 4, 1940, as the Pirates crushed the Boston Pilgrims, 14-2. Six more night games were played that summer, and were used by Benswanger as a "special attraction" that almost guaranteed large crowds because of their infrequent occurrences.

Just as radio broadcasts reached out to the public, so did night baseball. Many fathers and mothers were unable to attend games that began at 3:30 in the afternoon due to work or home commitments. With the addition of lights, families could watch Pirate games together in the spring, summer, and fall. No longer were the crowds at Forbes Field divided into men with hats and suits in one section, school children in the outfield, etc. Thus, baseball became associated with family, and Oakland and Forbes Field supported this atmosphere. Still, a few games under the lights were not enough to bring fans into Forbes Field on a consistent basis. Franklin Roosevelt would help to solve that problem.

In Europe, Germany had been at war since 1939, and their Japanese allies bombed Pearl Harbor in December 1941. The United States was fully involved in the war, with many young men traveling to Europe to battle the German forces. Thirty-eight days after the Pearl Harbor incident, Commissioner of Baseball Judge Kennesaw Mountain Landis asked President Roosevelt if baseball ought to be shut down during the war, knowing that

Americans' minds were focused on issues more important than a game. The following is Roosevelt's reply.

"I honestly feel that it would be best for the country to keep baseball going. There will be fewer people unemployed, and everybody will work longer hours and harder than ever before. And that means that they ought to have a chance for recreation and for taking their minds off work even more than before. Baseball provides a recreation which does not lasts over two hours or two hours and a half, and which can be enjoyed for very little cost. And, incidentally, I hope that night games can be extended because it gives an opportunity to the day shift to see a game occasionally. As for the players themselves, I know you agree with me that individual players of active military or naval age should, without question, enlist in the services. Even if the greater use of older players lowers the actual quality of the team, this will not dampen the popularity of the sport. [72]"

The president's ringing endorsement of the game, later known as the Green-Light Letter, enabled baseball to serve its stated purpose: entertainment. Baseball would continue to serve as an outlet for relaxation, allowing Americans to escape the pressures, hardships, and anxieties of the war, even if only for a short time. In Pittsburgh, fans clung to baseball as Roosevelt had predicted, responding well to the increased number of night games. Attendance at Forbes Field hovered around 500,000 during the 1941 and 1942 seasons, despite the presence of poor teams on the field, and increased to over 600,000 in 1943. Night games began to occur frequently at Forbes Field, just as Roosevelt had requested. Thus, the war elevated baseball to new levels of popularity, and in Pittsburgh, it changed the face of Oakland, making it a nighttime gathering place.

During the 1920s and 1930s, South Oakland had become a thriving hub of people and places to visit. Panther Hollow (aka Little Italy), beneath the center field wall, was the home of the DiNardo, Diulius, and several other Italian families. Just above the hollow on Bates Street, many small grocery stores were built, as were barber shops and shoe repair stores. A few blocks west, and on the other side of the hollow, residents began to crowd Dawson Street, Parkview Avenue, Ward Street, and Oakland Square. The hill above Fifth Avenue, just west of Pitt's buildings and Frank Nicola's Schenley Farms, was also becoming heavily populated as a middle-class Irish community. Oakland had quickly developed into a working-class residential area with strong ethnic ties. Still, the greatest growth in Oakland occurred along the area's dividing line, Forbes Avenue. Running parallel to Sennott Street (formerly known as Louisa Street) and Forbes Field, Forbes Avenue and its cross streets became Oakland's business district. Many restaurants had opened there, along with small boutiques. After prohibition was repealed in 1932, some bars opened in the area and were instantly successful. Neighborhood children were often seen selling newspapers on Forbes Avenue near the ballpark, and the street became a place to stroll along before and after baseball games.

However, by 1944, the appeal of baseball as a break from work, the war, and other worries began to fade. Despite a second-place finish by the Pirates, only

500,000 fans came to Forbes Field. A mediocre finish the following season was overshadowed by Germany's surrender and the bombing of Hiroshima and Nagasaki. The war was over, and hundreds of thousands of Americans would soon return home. Fans across the country anxiously awaited the arrivals of their favorite players who had served the nation. In Pittsburgh, a young minor leaguer also came home from the war and was poised to reinvigorate Forbes Field and the Oakland area. His name was Ralph Kiner.

CHAPTER 6: THE GOLDEN ERA?

In March 1946, twenty-three-year-old outfielder Ralph Kiner reported to the Pirates' spring camp in San Bernardino, California, with few expectations. After a torrid exhibition season in which he impressed all with his hitting, Kiner was invited to join the club in Pittsburgh as a member of the squad. Surprisingly, he led the National League in home runs that season with twenty-three, and word spread of his power. More than 700,000 fans came to Forbes Field that season, the most since the Pirates' last pennant-winning season in 1927. Still, the Bucs finished in seventh place, and two major disasters marred the season.

In mid-season, labor lawyer Robert Murphy attempted to organize major league players into the American Baseball Guild. He focused his early efforts in Pittsburgh, already a strong union town with its many steelworkers[73]. When the owners and Commissioner Happy Chandler would not entertain Murphy's demand for unionization, he asked the Pirates to go on strike. However, before a game at Forbes Field on June 8, 1946, the strike vote was defeated, in part because the players held Bill Benswanger in such high regard[74]. Although the strike never occurred, Benswanger was frustrated by its looming presence. This frustration was compounded by another battle between the Pirates' front office and the newspaper boys of the Pittsburgh papers. As a result, the Pirates were given much negative publicity. Benswanger and his mother-in-law were fed up with the current situation. It was time, they felt, to sell the Pirates and Forbes Field.

Mrs. Dreyfuss had quietly put the team up for sale prior to the strike and the newsboy incidents, but their occurrences hardened her resolve. Frank McKinney, a banker from Indianapolis who owned a minor league club there and held a ten percent stake in the Boston Braves, negotiated an option to purchase the Pirates and Forbes Field. He asked a Pittsburgh lawyer to become a part, serving as a local member. Soon, an ownership group was formed, with McKinney and Perlbrecht joining the syndicate, and Johnson was invited to buy ten percent of the group's shares. Note who had recently bought into the Cleveland Indians. By the end of July, McKinney's group had purchased Dreyfuss shares in the Pittsburgh Athletic Company (the Pirates) and the Forbes Field Company (Forbes Field) for roughly $2.25 million[75]. For the first time since 1900, the Dreyfuss name was no longer associated with Pittsburgh baseball.

One of the first decisions made by the new group was the hiring of Roy Hamey, a bright baseball executive, as the club's general manager. The four new owners were all dedicated to affairs outside of baseball, so Hamey's job was essentially to run the club. However, the flair of owning a major league team appealed to Frank McKinney, and he gradually began to take over the baseball operations. At his insistence, the other three owners purchased shares in the Indianapolis club from McKinney, allowing it to be linked to the Pirates. This became a poor relationship for the Bucs, as McKinney, being the majority owner, often sent established Pirates to Indianapolis to bolster that team, which was his true love.

Still, McKinney wanted to improve the Pirates, which he did by signing the legendary Hank Greenberg to a one-year deal, worth $40,000. Only such an exorbitant amount could keep Greenberg, a long-time Detroit Tiger hero, from retiring. Greenberg's signing coincided with the new owners' decision to repair Forbes Field. The ballpark, which was now thirty-eight years old, had become run-down, as Benswanger and Mrs. Dreyfuss spent little money on its upkeeping. The bathroom walls were filthy, covered with urine stains, and the seats in the grandstand were only seventeen inches wide[76]. The owners spent over $1 million to repair the bathrooms and replace the seats with twenty-two-inch ones. The backstop, which at one hundred ten feet was so far behind home plate that a speedy runner could score from second base on a passed ball, was moved thirty feet closer toward the plate.

The other major renovation at Forbes Field that winter was the addition of Greenberg Gardens, a thirty-foot-wide space between the left-field wall and the outfield. The owners relocated the two bullpens into the space, thereby decreasing the distance from the left field foul pole from a monstrous 365 feet to a more reasonable 335 feet. This was done to take advantage of Hank Greenberg's mighty right-handed bat, but Ralph Kiner was clearly the greatest beneficiary. Although Greenberg performed well that season, hitting twenty-five home runs, the Gardens were most kind to Kiner, who belted fifty-one, once again leading the National League.

Although the Bucs repeated their seventh-place performance of one season earlier, fans came in droves to Forbes Field in the summer of 1947, mainly to see Kiner come to bat. There is nothing more exciting in the game of baseball than the home run, and Kiner's performance proved that, as attendance climbed to 1,283,531. Despite the poor play of the rest of the club, Kiner's big bat captivated Pirate fans. "It was amazing," said teammate Frank Gustine, "If Ralph batted in the eighth, it seemed like the whole place would get up and leave afterward. But if there was a chance he would bat in the ninth, nobody left[77]."

In 1948, Billy Meyer was hired to manage the team, and Hamey made several off-season trades that created excitement before the opener. Most men had returned from the war, and people were beginning to re-adjust to life at home. The thrills Kiner provided fans in '47, combined with Hamey's personnel moves and the post-war excitement, generated great anticipation for the 1948 season. 38,546 filled Forbes Field on opening day, a new record for the ballpark[78]. The team played well, as Kiner once again led the league in home runs with forty. However, the Pirates could not win the pennant, finishing in fourth place, eight and a half games behind the St. Louis Cardinals. Despite Kiner's National League single-season best of 54 home runs in 1949, the Pirates fell to sixth place; yet, 1.5 million fans still came to Forbes Field to watch them.

It seemed as though Kiner's magic and the return of our soldiers created a sense of euphoria in the Oakland area. Many of the war veterans lived off what was known as the 52-20 club, which gave veterans $52 for every twenty weeks they spent in the service. As a result, many Oaklanders loafed around after returning home. This "club" also helped to increase attendance at the ballpark, which coincided with the tremendous growth in Oakland's popularity. Many new establishments began to prosper in the 1940s near Forbes Field and Forbes Avenue, giving Oakland's business district true life. Jack Cantor's restaurant, located at the corner of Forbes and Atwood Streets, became well-known for its corned beef sandwiches. Often, children sold newspapers outside his restaurant, and if they were having a bad day, he would give them a sandwich to brighten their spirits[79]. Peter Kunst opened a bakery nearby on Forbes Street on November 30, 1945. The bakery, bearing his name, was a welcome addition to the residents of South Oakland and outsiders alike. Other restaurants came to the area, including Thompson's, Weinstein's, Black Angus, the Clock, Devonshire, Cicero's, White Tower, Original Frank and Burger, Betsy Ross Tea Room, and Frank Blandy's Park Schenley restaurant, one of the city's finest. Matt Trabert's restaurant, which had opened earlier, began to attract more customers in the late 1940s. There, guests were lucky to receive what they ordered, thanks to an autocratic German waiter by the name of Biz Mim[80]. These establishments and others offered a great variety to patrons in Oakland, and all were blocks away from Forbes Field.

Several bars also prospered in the area, largely due to the presence of the ballpark. Pete Coyne opened his bar on Atwood Street, just two blocks west of Forbes Field, which enjoyed the benefits of night baseball. Sandscratchers was also on Atwood Street and served as an after-hours club for the men in the area. The Irish Club on Oakland Avenue was a haven for local Irishmen as well as their comrades of all ethnic backgrounds. The Oakland Cafe, another popular bar, was the site of many brawls. The Home Plate Cafe, opposite Forbes Field on Bouquet Street, was very popular before and after games at the park. These bars experienced increased patronage due to the rise in attendance at the ballpark, but were primarily frequented by Oakland natives.

The decade was also kind to several shops and other attractions on Forbes Avenue. Prices, a multi-purpose store, was across the street from Kunst Bakery. Binstock's jewelry store, Leonard Nadel's Men's Shop at the northern corner of Forbes and Bouquet, Shea's Sporting Goods, Gus Miller's Newsstand, Jack Dines' Cigar Shop, and other stores filled Oakland and enabled residents to fulfill virtually all of their needs within a few blocks. The Myers Printing Company served the publishing needs of the neighborhood and was located outside Forbes Field, along the left-field line. One block closer to Forbes Avenue was the Steel City Auto Company, a used car lot. There were also three movie theaters on Forbes Avenue (the Strand, the King's Court, and the Schenley), Stuckert's gas station on Forbes in front of the ballpark, a wine store, Hahn's card shop, Rosenblum's Tailors, and the famous Isaly's Ice Cream parlor. People often entered Oakland at 6:00 pm for a 7:30 pm game, leaving them time to peruse the area. Pie Traynor, the former third baseman and manager of the Pirates, now lived in the Schenley Apartments and walked the streets of Oakland, greeting everyone with a kind word. Children and adults alike enjoyed the variety of Oakland in a safe environment, day or night. By the end of the decade, Oakland was clearly a thriving business and residential community.

Even though these Oakland landmarks brought patrons to the area, Oakland clearly belonged to its residents. A unique blend of Jews, many of whom lived on McKee Place, Irish people in South Oakland and on Dunsieth Street up the hill near Pitt's campus, Italians in the Hollow, and African Americans on Center Avenue truly represented a diverse neighborhood. This area was well-equipped to deal with turbulence from outsiders, with the likes of Tommy Malko, who once beat up a thug from the South Hills at the corner of Forbes and Atwood for raising his voice to an older lady from Oakland. Joey Diven, another tough Oaklander, defended his friends in the neighborhood bars and acted as a bodyguard to famous people visiting the area[81]. Other characters in the area included Balloonhead Maloney, Jigs Joyce, Duck O'Donell, Softy Dougherty, and a man named McCallister the Whaler, whose loud, whaling noises filled the air at Forbes Field.

Although there were many attractions in Oakland aside from the ballpark, Forbes Field was still the area's finest drawing card. Some fans now drove to Oakland, finding parking spaces along both sides of Forbes Avenue, an open lot in front of the Park Schenley restaurant in Schenley Park, and even on the lawns of homes on side streets, for a nominal price[82]. Even still, many fans continued to arrive at the ballpark via streetcar. Ernie's and Tom & Jerry's hot dog stands on Bouquet Street offered fans an inexpensive bite to eat before a game. Qinque's, a small truck outside of the bleachers, offered similar amenities, and peanuts were sold nearby by a man known as "Preacher[83]."

While many customers who travelled to the game bought tickets to enter the park, the fans from Oakland often had more clever ways to see a game.

Children could sell papers for Gus Miller in exchange for a chance to see the Pirates, and Miller also appointed young Oakland men to usher. Those who collected the most foul balls and returned them to Miller were given a fifty-cent piece and allowed to usher in the next game[84]. Ditty Rittmeyer and friends scaled the wall at Forbes Field on Bouquet Street, climbing up to the third tier and making their way around to available seats. Tom "Maniac" McDonough was also a famous wall scaler; his prey, however, was the right field stands[85]. Other non-paying entrances included the gate for concession boss Myron O'Brisky on Bouquet Street, which was often left open. A gate for crippled people between the bleachers and stands often induced young Oaklanders to lose their ability to walk for a few minutes[86]. Other people would stand by the will-call window on Sennott Street, listen to the names of people for whom tickets were dropped off, and then claim to be those people a few minutes later[87]. Some people knew Red McCartney and the other Oaklanders who collected tickets at the gates and were allowed in for free. The remaining men from Oakland who did not use any of the above methods to get into the ballpark felt it was their birthright to enter Forbes Field. When asked if anyone from Oakland ever paid to see a game at Forbes Field, Big Bob DePasquale, a former usher at Forbes Field, replied, "In a word, no. We got guys who say they're from the IRS and they're looking for tax dodgers. We got guys who get old chauffeurs' hats and wrap up a big empty box and say they are making a delivery[88]." Often, excuses like these were good enough to get inside the ballpark.

Once in the park, Pirate fans were treated to Ralph Kiner's blasts and little else. Miserable baseball induced some fans to focus their attention on other activities once inside Forbes Field. A small contingent of gamblers occupied parts of the park, including a few rows in the second deck behind home plate, and a few more in the bleachers. Luke Barnett, among others, ran numbers from the stands, usually involving games of the day at Forbes Field and across the country[89]. However, their activities were only minor, as gambling never fully infiltrated Oakland as it had in other sections of the city. More appropriately, the stands were filled with characters who consistently labored through each game with the Pirates. Men like the "Professor," an old man in a suit who sat in the third row of the bleachers and provided a running analysis of the game, helped to ease the pain induced by the miserable play of the team[90].

Special events, such as Ladies Days, drew women to the ballpark.

Children could join the Knot-Hole Gang in the summertime, which entitled them to see certain Saturday games in the rightfield stands at no cost. John Fogerty took care of the playing field, keeping it hard so that ground balls would skip to the outfield quickly, thus aiding the poor Pirate bats. The view of Flagstaff Hill and Schenley Park was breathtaking for the fans in the upper decks, and despite the team's poor performance, fans continued to come. As the decade came to a close, Oakland, with its ballpark, was the city's biggest attraction and no longer its best-kept secret.

The 1950 season began no better than the previous one had ended. Frank McKinney continued to override Roy Hamey's decisions, and the quality of the team suffered. At the All-Star Game in Chicago that summer, Tom Johnson approached McKinney to discuss what he and John Galbreath had deemed an impossible ownership situation. Johnson offered McKinney his Indianapolis club back, in return for the right to purchase his shares in the Pittsburgh Athletic Company and the Forbes Field Company. McKinney agreed, and Johnson and Galbreath split McKinney's shares equally[91]. The change in ownership was not enough to assist the struggling Bucs, though, and the team finished in last place for he first time since 1917. Ralph Kiner led the league in home runs once again, but problems loomed. Attendance, while still high, had fallen below 1.2 million, and the time was ripe for more changes.

In the off-season, Branch Rickey, the general manager of the Brooklyn Dodgers who brought Jackie Robinson and the World Series to Brooklyn, was fired by Walter O'Malley. Rickey, who had a fine reputation, was also a fraternity brother of John Galbreath. By November, Rickey had mesmerized Galbreath with plans to rebuild the Pirates, and he was hired to replace Roy Hamey and run the team. In Pittsburgh, he proceeded to trade away young talents like Wally Westlake and Gus

Bell, who went on to have fine careers. He angered players with his rough tactics in contract negotiations and sent fans into an uproar by trading Ralph Kiner two months into the 1953 season. Kiner, who had led the league in home runs again in 1951 and 1952, was too high-priced for Rickey's liking, and the general manager reasoned that the club, now known as the Rickey Dinks, could finish in last place just as well without Kiner as they did with him[92]. Greenberg Gardens, which became known to some as Kiner's Korner, was removed, and the bullpens and fences were restored to their original positions after the 1953 season. Rickey soon became the target of media attacks, and his continued arrogant approach to his job did not sit well with Tom Johnson. While in New York for the 1955 World Series, Johnson asked Galbreath to go for a walk outside of Galbreath's apartment.

After thirty blocks, Johnson had convinced Galbreath that Rickey had to go and that Joe L. Brown, the man in charge of the Pirates minor league club in New Orleans, should replace him.

Although he was correct in his prediction about the Pirates' fate with or without Kiner, Rickey ignored the slugger's tremendous ability to bring fans to Forbes Field. Without Kiner, the team finished in last place from 1953 to 1955, but more importantly, attendance decreased to less than 500,000 fans per season. Ralph Kiner led the National League in home runs for a record seven consecutive seasons as a Pirate. He was a hero to nearly every young baseball fan in Pittsburgh, and many people resented his departure for years to come. Dale Long's streak of eight home runs in eight consecutive games added a spark to the 1955 season, but it was only a temporary cure for the Pirates' ailments. Without Ralph Kiner, much of the life that filled Forbes Field was gone.

Oakland was changing outside of Forbes Field as well. Many of the same young men who participated in the 52-20 club after the war were now getting married and moving away from Oakland. The homes in the area were clean but getting old, and were too close together. What was once a quiet area had become filled with shoppers, diners, drinkers, and fans from outside of Oakland. Young couples moved to suburbs like Brookline, North Hills, and Monroeville, where land was cheaper and more plentiful than in Oakland. The area was still the hub of the city's single Irish and Italian men, but they could not sustain a commercial center on their own. Once again, Oakland seemed ripe for another transition.

CHAPTER 7: TIMES OF CHANGE:

PITT AND THE RENAISSANCE

The post-World War II era at the University of Pittsburgh was one of remarkable importance to the school, the people of Oakland, and the entire city of Pittsburgh. By 1947, the University had become too crowded and not enough buildings were available, causing Rufus Fitzgerald, the chancellor from 1945-1955, to "hope that enrollment will go down.[93]" In April of that same year, Fitzgerald persuaded the Board of Trustees to create a Planning and Development committee, to be headed by current trustee Alan Magee Scaife.

Scaife was a wealthy man whose family had tremendous influence on all matters in Pittsburgh. His mother was a member of the Magee family, renowned for its connections to the hospital and political spheres, and his wife was Sarah Mellon, the daughter of banking magnate Richard B. Mellon, who, along with his brother, bankrolled numerous university and city projects. Fitzgerald knew that if anyone could raise enough money to aid the University, it was Alan Scaife. Scaife carefully considered the needs of the University and proposed the following plan: a new library, a residence hall, and a student center were essential to Pitt's growth, while a medical school, a science building, and a gym & athletic field house were necessary[94]. Scaife estimated the total cost of the projects to be $20 million. George Hubbard Clapp, the Chairman of the Board of Trustees, agreed to donate three million dollars, allowing Scaife's committee to proceed with its plans. However, despite the initial enthusiasm with which Scaife's plans were met, the reality set in that there was little land on which the University could build. Thus, Pitt was at a crossroads. It had become too large for the area it had occupied for forty years, but most of the surrounding land in Oakland was already being used for other purposes. If Pitt were to grow, it would have to expand into other parts of Oakland.

The most obvious available site on which the University could build was the lawns of the Cathedral of Learning. This was the largest unoccupied area owned by the University, but many considered its vacancy a benefit to the school and the city. Scaife's father-in-law, Richard B. Mellon, was opposed to building on the lawns because he wanted to preserve an open vista that was rare in the city[95]. Soon, many others opposed building on the lawns, and they were kept open as a tribute to the rural area that Oakland once was. The board maintained its vision of open land and explored other available properties.

Expansion was stalled by a lack of available sites for Scaife's proposed new buildings. In June 1950, Richard B. Mellon assisted the University in acquiring a three-acre plot on the north side of Fifth Avenue, across from the Cathedral. There, the engineering building, to be known as Clapp Hall, was built.

Property was also acquired adjacent to Pitt Stadium for the new field house. Under the guidance of new athletic director Thomas Hamilton, the field house was completed in 1951 with a seating capacity of 6,000, expandable to 8,000, a wrestling room, a 220-yard dirt track, and both training and locker rooms[96]. This was the last major act of expansion under Fitzgerald, as the chancellor retired after the 1955 academic year. Before he retired, Fitzgerald strongly emphasized the necessity to create more substantial professional schools at the University.

The expansion plans of Rufus Fitzgerald for the University were understood and elevated to a higher level under the leadership of Edward Litchfield, his successor. Litchfield, an idealist who had been the dean of Cornell's School of Business, wanted to elevate Pitt's academic reputation, placing it on par with Harvard and Yale as one of the finest institutions of higher learning in the world. Immediately, Litchfield increased the school's average expenditure per student and raised the quality of the University's faculty. Still, the area of expansion needed to be addressed.

Litchfield's first concern was that the University had too few residence halls. If Pitt was to become a great institution, he thought it was necessary to increase the available dormitory space so that more students could be encouraged to live on the campus. His initial action to rectify this situation came in December 1955, when he persuaded the Board of Trustees to purchase the Schenley Apartments from Frank Nicola's Bellefield Company. The apartments consisted of five buildings, 238 apartments, and 1,113 rooms, and were acquired by the University at a cost of approximately three million dollars. The school poured another million dollars into renovations to the buildings, which were opened for the 1957-58 academic year. Although the entrance to the apartments was on Fifth Avenue, the buildings extended south to Forbes Avenue. Thus, the purchase of the Schenley Apartments represented the University's continued expansion into the South Oakland region (the Cathedral was the first) and signaled Pitt's readiness to continue along these lines.

Just over one month later, Litchfield addressed the lack of an adequate student center, a concern first mentioned by Alan Scaife in his initial report to the board in 1947. The Board of Trustees acquired the grand Schenley Hotel, also owned by the Bellefield Company, for $1.8 million. The hotel, adjacent to the Schenley Apartments, was a major attraction from its construction in 1898 and remained popular in 1956, when it was sold to the University. By October 9, 1957, all major student activities were housed in the hotel. The top three floors were used as dormitories, and many of the remaining rooms had been remodelled. In just two years, Edward Litchfield had substantially improved residential and activity facilities at the University. Still, many more changes were necessary to make Pitt into one of America's leading institutions.

The University continued its purchasing spree in late 1957 when it acquired the Memorial Hospital from the city for $1.3 million. The building, renamed Jonas Salk Hall for the Pitt research giant who discovered the polio vaccine, also became home to the schools of dentistry and pharmacy. In February of 1958, Litchfield added to his growing residential facilities with the purchase of the Ruskin Apartments, on Fifth Avenue near Clapp Hall, for the purpose of future faculty residences. Dr. Litchfield's dreams for Pitt were beginning to take shape.

Earlier, in a speech to the Board in March 1957, Litchfield re-emphasized many of the items that Dr. Fitzgerald and Alan Scaife had seen as necessary for Pitt's success ten years prior. Litchfield was asking the state for money to support expansion of athletic facilities, classrooms, a library, a professional school quad, more dormitories, and, above all, land on which to build[97]. Construction on a gymnasium and swimming pool, later known as Trees Hall, began in early 1958 near the Field House and the Stadium on the hilltop.

Still, a large library was needed to replace the current facility that was cramped inside the Cathedral of Learning. In 1957 and 1958, the University purchased the Schenley Theatre, the Park Schenley Restaurant, the Zemmer Company Building, and the Joy Manufacturing Building so that the library could be built after they were razed[98]. The project was estimated to cost $10 million in total, with $3 million donated by trustee Henry Hillman. The other $7 million was pledged by the General State

Authority, which began to allocate increasingly high amounts of money to schools with a high number of in-state students. The launching of Sputnik I in the Soviet Union propelled many federal and state agencies throughout the country to invest in the education of Americans and ultimately, protection against the evils of Communism. So, the GSA's gift was consistent with those in other states at the time.

Concurrent with the University's expansion plans, the leaders of Pittsburgh's business and political worlds were in the process of making changes of their own in the city. As Oakland grew and prospered into a major civic center in Pittsburgh during the first half of the twentieth century, the downtown area began to decay. Steel, the city's largest industry and greatest asset, had become a liability, as the mills that produced it churned smoke and dust into the downtown air. Pittsburgh gained a reputation for being a dirty, second-class city, something that new Democratic Mayor David Lawrence sought to change.

Fortunately for the mayor, Richard K. "Dick" Mellon, a Republican, shared his desire to improve Pittsburgh. The wealthy son of Richard B., Dick Mellon, came home from the war with the attitude that he would use his money to better his city. However, Mellon's ability to influence other wealthy Pittsburghers as well as local business leaders was the key to Pittsburgh's facelift, known as the Renaissance. The Renaissance effort was spearheaded by the Allegheny Conference on Community Development (ACCD), an organization formed in 1944 with the express purpose of enhancing Pittsburgh and its surrounding regions. The ACCD, along with the Pittsburgh Regional Planning Association, which had existed for many years, gained significant power as its boards were filled with Pittsburgh's corporate leaders. Men like Gwilym Price of Westinghouse, Edgar Kaufmann of Kaufmann's Department Store, Henry Heinz of the H.J. Heinz Company, Clifford Hood of U.S. Steel, Leland Hazard of Pittsburgh Plate Glass, and Park Martin, among others, devoted time and money to these organizations.

Collectively, they hoped to increase the value of their companies by investing in their homes.

With the support of Dick Mellon and these other business leaders, Mayor Lawrence successfully embarked on a smoke-abatement program in the late 1940s. This program gave rise to other cleanup efforts downtown, and soon the ACCD had a plan for continued improvements throughout the city. Lawrence's Renaissance program attracted national attention, and with it, federal and state funds. The downtown area had become the poster child for the movement, and its continued improvement was critical to the success of the Renaissance. By the end of the 1940s, a public park had been built at the fork of the Allegheny, Monongahela, and Ohio Rivers. This masterpiece, known as Point State Park, was a shining example of the Renaissance's accomplishments. A wasted piece of land was transformed into an area of civic beauty.

Despite the Renaissance's emphasis on the downtown area, Oakland's development was also integral to the movement. Litchfield's high hopes for the

University of Pittsburgh aligned well with those of Mayor Lawrence and the ACCD. Surely, any great city must be a place where learning is stressed, and what better place to learn than the rapidly improving and prestigious University of Pittsburgh. The civic leaders also recognized the potential for Pitt's new Medical School, if properly connected to the existing hospitals nearby, to create an outstanding medical center for residents throughout Allegheny County and its surrounding areas. Thus, the ACCD and city politicians projected Oakland as the educational and medical hub of the region and did everything in their power to make this a reality. Clearly, though, athletic events in Oakland were not part of the plan for it's future.

Thus, Pitt's expansion into South Oakland was not discouraged by local politicians and business leaders. They realized, just as Litchfield did, that this was the natural progression of the University. Most of the land on the hill above Fifth Avenue was already used by the school, and only South Oakland remained immune to the long arm of the University. Expanding vertically was not a possibility due to concerns about excessive costs, similar to those incurred by the Cathedral of Learning. Pitt paid large amounts of money to acquire the Schenley buildings and the properties across the street for its future library; in essence, too much money for the owners of these properties to turn down. By 1958, after most of its neighbors had been purchased by the University, Forbes Field's existence was clearly threatened.

In Milwaukee, Wisconsin, the city and county governments collaborated to construct a large stadium with extensive parking facilities. Automobiles had become more prevalent by the 1950s, and people began to rely less on public transportation. Mayor Lawrence recognized the lack of available parking in Oakland for games at Forbes Field and knew that this problem, along with traffic congestion in the area, would only worsen over time. By 1955, rumors abounded throughout the region that a new municipal stadium was being planned in Pittsburgh. Lawrence wanted to give the city a new stadium, while at the same time continuing his Renaissance by rebuilding a dilapidated area in the city.

One part of Pittsburgh that had become nearly deserted was the North Side, the same area that once housed Recreation and Exposition Parks. Since the Pirates and other attractions left in 1909, many businesses had failed, and residents had moved out. Immigrants, who once chose the North Side as their home, were now locating in various other sections of the city or its suburbs. Much of the North Side was wasteland, with very little traffic running through it. This area seemed to be the next logical "project" in the Renaissance.

In Oakland, the Pittsburgh media and government officials began to paint a sour picture of the conditions at Forbes Field. Writers across the city felt that the Steelers would leave Pittsburgh unless they were given a new stadium in which to play. Forbes Field, they said, was no longer adequate for the increasingly popular game of football, with its limited seating capacity and poor sightlines. The media also presented to the public the idea that the Pirates were unhappy with Forbes Field and wished to play elsewhere. The public became worried that the two major sports teams in the city would leave if not given a new place to play. This sense of public insecurity, created by the media and the Lawrence administration, caused people to react with urgency to the stadium situation.

On March 19, 1958, a special meeting of the Executive Committee of Pitt's Board of Trustees was convened to propose that Pitt lease its stadium to the Public Auditorium Authority, who in turn would lease it to the Pittsburgh Steelers for five years, with the ability for either party to cancel the lease on one year's notice[99]. This would provide the Steelers with a temporary home until the much-discussed municipal stadium was ready for play, keeping the team in the city and providing fans with a slight sense of relief. However, it was also made clear that this lease would not be renewed under any circumstances at the end of the five-year period.

In April 1957, a group of students from Carnegie Tech, in cooperation with the North Side Civic

Promotion Council, investigated the items necessary to keep the professional baseball and football teams in Pittsburgh permanently. They also attempted to determine if these items were available at Forbes Field and/or Pitt Stadium (although neither the Pirates nor the Steelers played any games at Pitt Stadium, it was the city's largest facility, and its future use was unclear)[100].

This committee was followed by one appointed by the Commissioners of Allegheny County and Mayor Lawrence on February 27, 1958, to study and report on the need and feasibility of the construction of a multi-purpose sports stadium to serve the greater Pittsburgh area[101]. The committee submitted its written report on September 1, 1958. In the report, the committee initially determined that Forbes Field was no longer adequate for several reasons. First, the University of Pittsburgh was developing rapidly and successfully in Oakland, an area that was geographically small. There simply was not enough room, physically, for Pitt to continue to develop naturally in the fields of education and medicine if sports were to remain in the Oakland area.

Secondly, Forbes Field's and Oakland's lack of parking facilities in general was becoming a significant problem because people were becoming more inclined to drive to a game there, rather than take public transportation. The committee also stressed that Forbes Field was not suited for multi-purpose use, nor was Pitt Stadium. This, coupled with the fact that both facilities were over thirty years old, led the committee to conclude that renovations to either were not the answer. In general, the committee's evaluation stressed Forbes Field's impediment to the necessary growth of education and medicine in Pittsburgh.

The committee also claimed that if Forbes Field continued to be the home of professional sports in Pittsburgh, these teams would leave the city.

Next, the committee proposed nine potential sites for a multi-purpose, municipal stadium. The committee recommended a site on the North Side, on Monument Hill. They proceeded to analyze the advantages of this site and projected costs for the project. It was assumed that the University of Pittsburgh would be interested in using the new municipal stadium. The city realized that professional sports teams were essential to keep residents in Pittsburgh and attract tourists, providing an influx of capital to the hotels, restaurants, and stores in the city. The report was made public immediately.

Just before the report was released, Pirates majority owner John Galbreath was called downtown to meet with a committee of three (Ed Magee was one of the three; the others are believed to be Leon Falk and Frank Denton, both Trustees of Pitt). This committee asked Galbreath to sell Forbes Field, catching him off guard. He explained that Forbes Field was a good park and that the team was doing well financially playing there. The men proceeded to tell Galbreath that Chancellor Litchfield wanted Forbes Field to be the site for Pitt's new graduate schools. When Galbreath explained that he was not interested, one of the men said, "Well, would you be interested if we (the city and the county) built you a new stadium...on a very good site, and it wouldn't cost you a dime?[102]" When the site was explained to be across from Point State Park on the North Side, and the stadium's capacity was estimated at 52,000, Galbreath quickly changed his mind. He would confer with his partners, but was fairly certain that a deal could be reached with the University to sell Forbes Field.

Pitt had hoped for some time that Forbes Field would become available. Chancellor Litchfield first mentioned this possibility at the board's meeting on June 10, 1958[103]. The board began negotiating with John Galbreath, Tom Johnson, and their attorneys in early November 1958, and a plan for purchasing the ballpark was presented to the executive committee at its meeting at the Duquesne Club on November 13, 1958. The University would purchase the land and building, totaling 6.5 acres, from the Forbes Field Company for $3 million, or only $7.22/square foot. The University would then lease the ballpark to the club at $150,000/year for five years. At the end of the five-year period, the Pirates would move to the new municipal stadium on the North Side, if it were built, or the team would remain at Forbes Field at $150,000/year until it was built[104]. All of the committee members present were in favor of the proposal. The negotiations were made public on November 28, 1958, in a statement released by the University. The entire board resolved the proposal on December 9, 1958.

Although the owners of the Pirates were happy at Forbes Field and in Oakland, they did not want to be known as the men who blocked Pitt's progress. Pressure from the city and the ACCD to sell Forbes Field, along with a promise to build a new facility free of charge within the next five years, helped clinch their decision. Forbes Field was now a part of the University of Pittsburgh, but it remained the home of the Pittsburgh Pirates.

CHAPTER 8: HOW SWEET IT IS!

Upon learning of the sale of Forbes Field to the University of Pittsburgh, fans had mixed reactions. Many were excited about the prospect of a beautiful new stadium near the Golden Triangle. Those same people were the ones who pointed out the deficiencies of Forbes Field, citing its primitive structure. The park was filled with old iron girders, and steel supports blocked the view from certain seats. The clubhouses had no conveniences and looked like stables. The stench of beer on the floors at the ballpark was constant, and the lack of available parking was a large problem[105]. As far as they were concerned, it was time for a change.

Yet, many others were bitter about the sale. "Let Pitt move, not Forbes Field," said angry Oaklanders. The ballpark had become a meeting place for them and represented all that was good. The breathtaking view in the outfield, the rustling of the crowd outside in anticipation of the game, and even the rocks in the infield each contributed to the charm of Forbes Field. Business owners recognized that the loss of the ballpark would have a significant financial impact on them. Forbes Field had become the focus of Oakland, and its absence would surely leave a void in the lives of its devoted patrons.

Realistically, though, most people understood what was happening in Oakland. They loved Forbes Field and appreciated it as a classic facility, but also recognized that the ballpark was outdated. The amount of money necessary to modernize it was ludicrous, and even then, parking and traffic problems would still exist. While Forbes Field was certainly capable of continuing to house athletic events, it's future was bleak. As Pitt began to buy the properties surrounding the ballpark, people knew that Forbes Field would be next. Thus, while some people were in shock when the sale was announced and knew it would be sad to say goodbye to the ballpark, most understood that the time was right for change.

However, the loss of Forbes Field was not imminent, as the new municipal stadium was still being planned and was not expected to be built before the 1964 season.

Although the Steelers moved their home games to Pitt Stadium, Forbes Field remained the home of the Pirates.

Joe Brown replaced Branch Rickey as the Pirates' General Manager before the 1956 season. He inherited a number of talented players from Rickey and Hamey's labors, such as Roberto Clemente and Dick Groat, and acquired others to complement them. However, he made a major mistake by hiring Bobby Bragan as the manager in 1956. Bragan was too critical of the young players, and the team responded poorly, finishing seventh. The following season was even worse, as the club tied for last place despite having so much talent. Bragan was fired and replaced by first base coach Danny Murtaugh on an interim basis. The Bucs played better under Murtaugh, a former Pirate utility infielder, and he was retained.

In 1958, the Pirates finished in second place, drawing 1.3 million fans to Forbes Field, and the future looked bright. A parade was held downtown for the team, and excitement built around Pirate baseball. After the season, Joe Brown traded Frank Thomas, a slugger who hit thirty-five home runs that year, to Cincinnati for third baseman Don Hoak, catcher Smokey Burgess, and pitcher Harvey Haddix. This trade, combined with those that brought center fielder Bill Virdon to the Pirates from the Cardinals, catcher Hal Smith from the Athletics, and first baseman Rocky Nelson to the team, made the Pirates viable contenders for the pennant. Although the club finished in fourth place in 1959, attendance remained over 1.3 million. Fans flocked to Frankie Gustine's restaurant and bar across from the ballpark on Forbes Avenue. Pirates, their opponents, sportswriters, and fans gathered there before and after games, talking baseball and looking at the images of Pie Traynor, Honus Wagner, Paul Waner, and other Pittsburgh sports legends on the walls. Gustine, a former Pirate All-Star, greeted every customer who stepped through the door and knew most by name. The atmosphere at his establishment made it a popular one, and the collectibles inside served to remind Pirate fans of the days of championship baseball. The fans of Pittsburgh hungered for another World Series, and the time had arrived.

The Pirates won twenty-three games in their final at-bat in 1960, as the team got more out of its ability than any before it[106]. By the end of the summer, the team's confidence overflowed as the National League pennant returned to Pittsburgh for the first time since 1927. Murtaugh motivated his players, Don Hoak's fighting spirit set an example to his teammates, Dick Groat and Roberto Clemente had banner years, and Vernon Law won the Cy Young Award as the league's finest pitcher. A record 1,705,828 people attended Forbes Field during the 1960 regular season, as fans appreciated the comeback heroics of their Pirates. Clearly, no one believed in the team any more than the Gunner.

Bob Prince, affectionately known as "The Gunner", first appeared on the Pittsburgh baseball scene during the 1947 season as an assistant to broadcaster Rosey Roswell. Prince took over as the lead announcer when Roswell died in 1951, and followed in his predecessor's path as the team's biggest fan. Like Roswell, Prince could relate well to fans, but he was more of an entertainer than Rosey. Prince knew how to tell a story, but could also describe a baseball game with clarity and precision. His unmistakably raspy voice was immediately recognizable and was very reassuring to all.

Outside of the broadcast booth, the Gunner was still very much a character. Often clad in a bright, summery shirt, plaid sport coat, and $500 Gucci shoes with no socks, his outlandish style was matched by his unique sayings over the microphone[107]. Prince exclaimed, "You can kiss it goodbye," when a home run was hit, "He picked that up like a Hoover Sweeper," when a Pirate cleanly fielded a ground ball, "All we need here is a bloop and a blast," when the Pirates needed a rally, and "We had 'em all the way," after the Pirates edged an opponent[108]. Bob Prince's popularity grew during the 1950s as he sought to make boring games more engaging experiences. By the end of the decade, many fans attended games at Forbes Field with a radio in hand, simply to hear Prince describe the game they were watching. People fell in love with his antics on the air as well as his generosity. No autograph-seeker was turned away, and no charity snubbed if Bob Prince had a say in the matter. Bob Prince and his followers believed that the

Pirates could bring the championship of baseball back to their beloved city of Pittsburgh.

Still, a great challenge awaited the Pirates in the World Series, where their opponents would be the New York Yankees, winners of five of the previous ten summer classics. The Bronx Bombers' roster included Yogi Berra, Tony Kubek, Whitey Ford, Roger Maris, and Mickey Mantle, not to mention other stars. Certainly, the task ahead of the Pirates was a formidable one. The initial test took place on October 5, 1960, at Forbes Field during game one of the series. The ballpark looked beautiful as 36,667 fans came to see the first World Series game at the park in thirty-three years. A batting cage actually stood in the deepest part of center field (457 feet), as it was not collapsible. Very few people could reach it, or the flagpole in center field, which was also in play. A granite monument to Barney Dreyfuss stood near the wall in center field as a tribute to the former owner and creator of the ballpark. The grass was green, and the infield filled with dirt, sand, cinder, and rocks. Bob Prince added to his arsenal of sayings by exclaiming, "Beat 'em Bucs," a phrase that drew national attention[109].

Pirate fans sang a song entitled "The Bucs are going all the way," and Prince invented the Green Weenie, a piece of green plastic that mimicked concessionaire Myron O'Brisky's hot dogs, which Pirate fans shook at their opponents to jinx them. The team and the town were ready. The World Series was on!

5. Gate one of the 1960 World Series at Forbes Field.

In game one, the Pirates edged the Yankees, 6-4. Pirate second baseman Bill Mazeroski smacked a home run in the fourth inning, and Vernon Law and Elroy Face combined to pitch in the victory. In the second game, the fans at Forbes Field were not so lucky. The Yankees clobbered the Pirates, 16-3, behind two home runs from the switch-hitting Mantle. The third game was no better for the Bucs, as they were shut out back in the Bronx by Whitey Ford, 10-0. Luckily for the Pirates, it was Vernon Law's turn in the rotation for game four at Yankee Stadium. Law gave up only two runs in six and two-thirds innings, as Bill Virdon provided the offensive punch for the Pirates. Elroy Face closed the door on the Yankees over the final two and two-thirds innings, and would do the same in game five, a 5-2 Pirate victory. The Bucs left New York with the rest of the nation in a state of bewilderment and a one-game edge in the series.

The 38,580 fans who hoped to see the Pirates win the series in game six at Forbes Field were disappointed. Whitey Ford shut the Bucs out again, this time 12-0. Danny Murtaugh would not allow the beating to affect his team's preparation for game seven, saying, "The last time I checked the rule book, they were still settling the World Series on games won or lost, not on total runs."110 Murtaugh anointed Vernon Law as his starter for Game Seven, but the Pirates' ace was no longer effective. He could not hold a 4-0 lead early, and the Yankee bats also foiled the usually reliable Face. The Pirates came to bat in the bottom of the eighth inning, down 7-4.

Geno Cimoli, a Pirate reserve, batted for Face to begin the eighth and singled. Bill Virdon followed with what appeared to be an easy double play grounder to shortstop, but the ball hit a stone in the infield, changed directions, and struck Kubek in the throat, keeping the Pirate rally alive. This was typical of the infield at Forbes Field, which Bob Prince justifiably dubbed "The Alabaster Plaster[111]". Dick Groat properly thanked the infield for its kindness by smacking a single to left, scoring Cimoli, and putting the tying run on base. This prompted Yankee manager Casey Stengel to remove his starter, left-hander Bobby Schantz, and replace him with Jim Coates. Bob Skinner sacrificed the runners to second and third base respectively, and Rockey Nelson flied to right for the inning's first out. Roberto Clemente beat out a Baltimore chop to first base, as Coates was late to cover the bag, and Virdon scored, pushing the Bucs to within a run. 112 Hal Smith followed with a blast to left-center field for a home run, giving the Pirates a 9-7 lead. The crowd went crazy, and Smith's teammates jumped up and down in the dugout. The Pirate bats were silent for the remainder of the inning, but took a lead into the ninth.

Murtaugh turned the game over to Bob Friend, who promptly gave up two singles to open the inning. He was replaced by Harvey Haddix, who fared no better, giving up a run-scoring single to Mantle and a fielder's choice to Berra that scored the tying run. However, Haddix was able to thwart another Yankee attack, and the score remained tied, 9-9, with the Pirates coming to bat in the bottom of the ninth inning. Ralph Terry threw a ball to Pirate second baseman Bill Mazeroski to start the ninth. On his next pitch, Terry hung a high fastball to the stocky, slick-fielding Mazeroski and paid dearly for it.

Maz sent the ball over the left field wall at Forbes Field to give the Pirates the victory and the World Series title. He proceeded to rip his helmet off his head, waving it to the crowd as he rounded first base, a display of emotion that was rare for Mazeroski. 113 Several fans piled onto the field, rounding the bases with Mazeroski as he proceeded toward home plate. Domenic Varratti, an usher on the first base side that day, was beside himself as he rushed onto the field to greet the second baseman at the plate. Varratti had grown up on Bouquet Street and became friendly with Mazeroski at a young age, playing games such as "odds & evens" with him outside of the ballpark. 114 His rejoicement at the heels of Mazeroski served to further demonstrate the connection between the fans, the ballpark, and the Pirates, now the World Champions of baseball.

Mazeroski's blast marked the first time that the seventh game of the World Series had ended with a home run. Such a monumental achievement required an appropriate celebration, and the people of Pittsburgh responded accordingly. Hordes of fans raced by the Mary Schenley (aka, the Turtle Spit) fountain in search of the home run baseball, and the rest poured out into the streets. Soon, it seemed as if the entire population of Pittsburgh entered the downtown area, parading around the streets, throwing confetti, and celebrating for hours. By early evening, political officials begged people to avoid coming downtown, and the two tunnels connecting Pittsburgh to the South Hills were closed. 115 The people of Pittsburgh had finally been given another World Series title, and those who endured the thirty-five-year spell since the last one knew to celebrate accordingly.

Although the 1960 season and its climax took the minds of fans off the eventual closing of Forbes Field, the ensuing years did little to alleviate their concerns. The Bucs never finished higher than fourth place in the next few seasons after the 1963 season. The municipal stadium, which was to have been completely built on the North Side, remained a plan rather than a reality. Financial difficulties at the University of Pittsburgh, combined with the continued exodus of young men and women from Oakland residences, created a feeling of confusion and turmoil in the area.

"10. Bill Mazeroski's home run to win the 1960 World Series at Forbes Field."

CHAPTER 9: FAREWELL

While the Pirates fell to the bottom of the National League standings in 1963, the plans for their new home were being finalized. The Allegheny Conference on Community Development took the lead in the project, building on the recommendations of the joint City-County Stadium Study Committee, established on September 1, 1958. The conference leaders, particularly Ed Magee, were eager to begin construction of the new facility on the North Side in 1963, so that it would be available for the 1964 baseball season. Magee requested a meeting in 1962 to formally propose a new stadium to the Board of Commissioners of Allegheny County. At that meeting, one of the commissioners became extremely agitated by the fact that Magee and the other members of the ACCD had not initially presented this proposal to the city council, as the stadium was to be located within city limits. The board, following the insistence of Commissioner Dr. William McClelland, refused to discuss the matter until the plan was presented to the City Council[116].

City Council almost immediately ratified the plan, and it was brought back to the County Commissioners in an open meeting. When presented with the plans for financing the stadium, Dr. McClelland became very upset. These plans called for the taxpayers of the City of Pittsburgh and Allegheny County to bankroll the stadium, without any contributions from large corporations, the Pirates, or the Steelers. Dr. McClelland could not understand why the Pirates were not asked to invest the 3 million dollars they received for Forbes Field, at the very least. He was unaware that John Galbreath and Tom Johnson had been promised a new stadium for nothing if they sold Forbes Field to Pitt, and he was quite disturbed by this revelation[117].

McClelland's opposition to the proposed financing for the new stadium created a tremendous controversy. Political and business leaders alike believed that the commissioner should allow the project to proceed. Even Richard K. Mellon, the man largely responsible for the

Renaissance but typically un-opinionated about the stadium, thought McClelland was blocking progress and should step aside. McClelland persuaded John Galbreath to solicit funds from the industrial leaders of Pittsburgh to build the stadium, just as August Busch had done successfully in St. Louis a few years earlier. Galbreath attempted to collect money, but after two weeks came up with nothing and ceased the search. After all, he was promised a new stadium for free, and despite McClelland's protests, he felt he would soon have one.

McClelland's opposition substantially delayed the construction of the stadium. Under normal circumstances, this delay would have severely impaired the University's expansion plans, as Pitt could not use the Forbes Field property until the new stadium was ready for the Pirates. However, these were not normal times at Pitt, where financial problems were mounting. Chancellor Edward Litchfield's bold expansion program, which continued through 1958, cost more than $45 million. In the ensuing years, Litchfield severely overestimated the university's income in his budgets, which resulted in an accumulated deficit of more than $11 million from 1959 to 1963. Despite warnings from his top assistants and Gwilym Price, the Chairman of the Board of Trustees at the University, Litchfield continued to spend without limitation. He brought top professors to Pitt and attempted to build the finest facilities to attract more of their colleagues. Although Litchfield's expansion of the University's aspirations was made with good intentions, his actions were too bold. Some of his ideas included converting Pitt Stadium to a multi-purpose facility that could serve as the new municipal stadium for the city, filling in the giant Panther Hollow to allow for the construction of buildings on top, and a $250 million research complex that would extend horizontally inside the Hollow. Each of these ideas was eventually rejected, and the University simply could not honor many of the other commitments and projects Dr. Litchfield had agreed to undertake. By 1964, even Litchfield himself, usually the eternal optimist, admitted that he had erred in his planning of the budgets and that cut-backs were necessary. Still, he blamed the problems on the lack of fulfillment of a $125 million pledge by his friend and former Trustee, Alan Scaife, who died before this pledge was placed in his will[118]. Nevertheless, Pitt was in dire straits. After borrowing millions from several life insurance companies and obtaining second and third mortgages on many University buildings, including the Cathedral of Learning, no individual or corporation was willing to risk any more money on a school whose finances were so poorly managed.

Luckily for the University, the State of Pennsylvania was able to provide immediate assistance. Edward Litchfield admitted his mistakes, took ill, and resigned his chancellorship, and Stanton Crawford replaced him in the interim. After Crawford, Price, and other trustees convinced state politicians that the University was vital to the economic growth of Western Pennsylvania, Governor William Scranton provided $5 million in emergency aid to Pitt in July 1965. Price and Frank Denton, another trustee who also served on the Board of the Pirates and ran Mellon Bank, recognized the greater need for funds if Pitt was to balance its budget and remain expansive yet solvent in the future. The best alternative, they felt, was for the University to become a state-related institution. Following a study by a State House Sub-Committee and the Ford Foundation, Pitt was proclaimed a state-related school on August 23, 1966. The state increased its annual appropriation to Pitt substantially, and the University became eligible for General State Authority construction grants for academic buildings. The state was given the permanent right to appoint twelve people to Pitt's Board.

This move benefited the University and the state jointly, allowing Pitt to expand both in physical size and enrollment as well. The state mandated that tuition for in-state students be dramatically reduced, thus allowing enrollment to double in five years. At the same time, the size of the physical plant tripled. Dr. Wesley Posvar, a Colonel in the Air Force and professor at the Academy, was named Chancellor on January 13, 1967, and entered a more financially stable University. On March 27, 1968, as Dr. Posvar was inaugurated, the Hillman Library was dedicated adjacent to Forbes Field.

Unfortunately for the residents of Oakland, Pitt's new status brought even greater changes to the neighborhood. More money from the state meant more money for Pitt to expand, and lower tuition meant a rise in enrollment.

The influx of students created a need for more off-campus housing, and the University acquired many homes south of Forbes Avenue on Bouquet Street, Oakland Avenue, Atwood Street, and Meyran Avenue for this purpose. Those residents who sold their homes to the University were paid well, and those who refused eventually changed their minds after witnessing the conduct of their new neighbors. Students who had no permanent interest in the area and rented the homes had little concern for the upkeep of the community. Sidewalks were soon filled with pizza boxes and other pieces of trash, and the area that residents had taken such pride in for many years was becoming a "student ghetto. [119]"

The late 1960s and early 1970s were years of widespread protest across America, and Pittsburgh was certainly not immune to such activities. The Vietnam War and the Civil Rights Movement both encouraged students at Pitt to voice their opinions and represent an emerging counterculture. Students began to dress differently, wear their hair in new styles, use drugs more frequently, and soon called for revolutions. Protests occurred, both in University buildings and the streets of Oakland, as Bobby Kennedy and Martin Luther King Jr. were assassinated. Oakland, once a place of colorful characters, was now, according to its residents, a place of freaks[120].

Downtown, Dr. McClelland had been ousted by 1968, and plans to build the new stadium on the North Side were set to proceed. On April 24, 1968, ground was broken at the site; however, excavation costs proved more expensive than planned, leading to further discussions and delays. By 1969, construction was underway, and it seemed as if Pitt could finally demolish the building it had purchased eleven years earlier.

The municipal stadium, named "Three Rivers" for its position at the fork of the Allegheny, Monongahela, and Ohio Rivers, was set to open on July 16, 1970, when the Pirates would return home from a two-week road trip to face the Cincinnati Reds.

Before the team left for their trip to the West Coast, the final games were to be played at Forbes Field on June 28, 1970, quite fittingly in the form of a doubleheader against the Chicago Cubs, the Bucs' opponent in the inaugural game at the ballpark. The Pirates were having quite a season thus far under the guidance of Danny Murtaugh, who returned to manage them again at the

147

start of the season. On that final Sunday afternoon, Bill Mazeroski, still a hero in a town that could never forget him, recorded the last out of a Pirate sweep by gloving a grounder and touching second base in familiar fashion.

Thousands of fans stormed the field, equipped with the cutters that Bob Prince had advised them to bring, so that they might carry home a souvenir. People swarmed the scoreboard, grabbing the portable numbers that were used to display the score at Forbes Field and for games elsewhere. Still others attempted to pull seats from their foundations, in what had become a scene of hysteria. As people desperately attempted to cling to their memories of Forbes Field, they savagely tore it apart, destroying some of the beauty it had provided them.

Shortly thereafter, the University publicly released its plans to build the "Forbes Quadrangle" on the Forbes Field site, as well as many surrounding homes. Just as Pitt was about to proceed with the demolition of the ballpark, their plans were halted. Pete Flaherty, the mayor of Pittsburgh, quickly responded to the concerns of Oakland residents who felt threatened by the University's continuous expansion. Flaherty aligned with these citizens in what was recognized as an Anti-Pitt movement and used his influence to immediately disrupt Pitt's plans. He required the University to meet with every South Oakland organization in a community forum, where together they produced a charette for the area's future. Several additional community meetings took place, and Pitt was compelled to demonstrate to the people of Oakland how the new buildings would enhance the neighborhood. The University was required to confine its expansion to the Forbes Field site and thus redesign its plans for the Quadrangle.

In early 1971, Pitt's architects created a new design for the buildings, but demolition of the ballpark was halted once again. Eugene "Jeep" DePasquale, a member of the City Council representing South Oakland and former head of the union of ushers at Forbes Field, assisted a group of architectural professors and students from Carnegie Mellon University (formerly Carnegie

Tech) in presenting a plan to Pitt that would preserve Forbes Field forever.

The plan called for the stands to remain intact, with small homes built underneath them, victory gardens in the outfield, and Pitt's lecture halls on the infield. The University was required by Flaherty to seriously consider this plan, but was able to persuade him and DePasquale that the plan was foolish. The University needed to establish adequate professional schools for itself and for all of Western Pennsylvania, and the Forbes Field site was where it intended to carry out its plans. The politicians eventually agreed, but insisted that the University take some responsibility to maintain South Oakland as an adequate residential and commercial district. In cooperation, the University helped to form the Oakland Development Fund, which provided new housing in the area. Out of the struggle came strong dialogue between University officials and community organizations. Sandy Phillips, head of the People's Oakland organization, and others like her were able to communicate more effectively with Dr. Jack Freeman, an assistant to Dr. Posvar and later Vice President of Finance at the University, and other school officials. For the first time in years, the University of Pittsburgh pledged to no longer ignore the needs of the people of Oakland.

With tempers calm and the future seemingly clear, the University of Pittsburgh was able to proceed with its plans to destroy Forbes Field. On October 12, 1971, the sports world's focus shifted to the North Side of the city at Three Rivers Stadium, where the Pirates faced the Baltimore Orioles in the third game of the World Series. At the same time in Oakland, Forbes Field was being methodically picked apart, slammed with a headache ball, and bulldozed.

By 1975, Oakland was a vastly different place than it had been at the dawn of the decade. Most of the remaining remnants of the community were absorbed by the University of Pittsburgh, which ultimately came to dominate the area.

Forbes Street - Oakland's Business Strip
KEY: BOLD EDUCATION (PITT)
Italics Medicine (Doctors)

	1950	1958	1960	1970	1975
Meyran Ave. Int.					
3600	Laundromat	Dr.s Offices	Dr.s Offices / AE Phi Sorority	Dr.s Offices	Dr.s Offices
3604	Iroquois Apartments	Apts. & Few Offices	Dr.s Offices Few Offices	Dr.s Offices	
3610	Kunt's Bakery	Kunt's Bakery	Kunt's Bakery	Kunt's	Kunt's
3615	Edwards Bar &Strand Theatre	Strand Theatre	Strand	Strand Theatre	Theatre
Atwood St. Int.					
3701	Leanord's Mens	Leanord's Mens	Leanord's Mens	Leanord's	Leanord's
3702	Binstock's Jewelry	Suzan's women's	Suzan's womens	Record Store	Restaurant
3708	Weinstein's Rest.	Weinstein's Rest.	Weinstein's Rest.	Hungarian Village	McDonalds
3709	Edward's Barbers	Edward's Barbers	Edward's Barbers	VACANT	NA
3712	Oakland Café	Oakland Café	Oakland Ave. Int.	2 Resid.	Record Shop
Oakland Ave. Int.					
Bouquet St. Int.		(FORBES FIELD ENTRANCE ON BOUQUET & PARALLEL ST.)			
3901	Beauty Salon &	Auto Store &	Original Rest. & Residences(aka, "O")	"O"	"O"
3903	Residences	Residences	Residences	Sam Clothes	Record Store
3909	Flower Shop	Flower Shop	Flower Shop	**Pitt Rest.**	**Pitt Rest**
3911	College Café	Gustine's	Gustine's	Gustine's	Gustine's
3936	Stuckert's Gas	Stuckert's Gas	Stuckert's Gas	**Univ of Pgh**	**U of P**
	& Service	& Service	& Service	**Admin. Bldg.**	**Admin**
3941	Watch Repair	VACANT	Women's Sho p	**Univ.Shop**	**UnivShop**
3949	DeLuca Dresses	Book Store	Book Store	Marvins Mens Shop	Marvins **Univ Card Shop**
3950	White Tower	White Tower	White Tower	White Tower	**Pit Construction**
3953	Schenley Coffee Shop	Schenley Barber U of P Offices	Schenley Barber U of P Offices **U of P**	**Schenley** Traval	**U of P**
3954	Sporting Goods	Sporting Goods	Sporting Goods	**Pitt Library**........	
3960 -62	Schenley Theatre & Deli	Schenley Theatre & Deli	Constracation	**Pitt Library**........	
Pennant Pl. Int.					
3968	NA	Park Schenley Rest	Park Schenley Rest	**Pitt Library**........	
4027	Schenley Hotel	**Pitt Student Union**...			
4101 -51	**Pitt's**				
	Cathedral of Learning..				

Fast-food establishments crowded Forbes and Fifth Avenues, where ethnic restaurants once stood, because the families who frequented them had moved away, replaced by students with little time to spare. The medical center continued to expand, becoming one of the world's leading transplant centers. Forbes Avenue became a one-way street away from downtown, and Fifth Avenue became one-way as it entered town, forming thoroughfares and decreasing the number of available parking spaces in the area. This action also made it difficult to access certain stores, forcing shoppers to drive around blocks just to get near their destinations. Frankie Gustine's restaurant continued to operate, generating revenue despite the loss of Forbes Field. Frankie didn't stay long, though, choosing not to witness the transformation of a place he loved; instead, he opened a hotel in the suburbs. By the 1980s, Gustine's was gone from Oakland.

The destruction of Forbes Field, which began in 1971, was not completed until 1973 due to further issues with the plans for the site's new buildings. The University of

Pittsburgh announced its final plans to build Forbes Quadrangle on the Forbes Field property in January 1976, and the building was dedicated two years later. The Law School was built on Forbes Avenue, attached to the Quadrangle by way of a walking bridge that spanned Forbes Avenue and connected to the Schenley Apartments and Litchfield Towers. Mervis Hall, the graduate business school, was built in right-center field and dedicated in 1983. As a gesture of goodwill, the University preserved the home plate in glass inside Forbes Quadrangle's lobby, just a few feet from its original position, which would have kept it in a bathroom. The University also allowed a sizable portion of the left field wall to remain in its original position, with the distance markers and flagpole still intact. The red bricks of the wall are still covered by the ivy that graced them years ago.

Oakland, once a land of lush grass and cow pastures, has undergone dramatic changes since its inception. Once the domain of Mary Schenley, it became the object of Frank Nicola's vision for a model city. Soon, Oakland was transformed into a haven for the working class, and then slowly evolved into a diverse and busy neighborhood. Today, Oakland is completely dominated by the educational and medical facilities of the University of Pittsburgh. University buildings have replaced residences, and the population has decreased dramatically. Many of the businesses in the area that once employed residents are now gone, and most of Oakland's workers come from elsewhere. Foot traffic is sparse, making business even worse for those stores that remain. The student shopper is now the catered-to customer. Kunst Bakery, whose former services were strictly retail, remains open but survives largely as a wholesaler, providing baked goods to the cafeterias of the hospitals in the medical center.

Much of the culture that graced Oakland is gone. The Syria Mosque was purchased by the University and destroyed in 1990; the symphony and the opera left with it, relocating downtown to the new Heinz Hall. The Carnegie Institute and the Phipps Conservatory remain, but they now exist as outcasts in a place where they were once the center of attention.

The nightlife in Oakland is dominated by students, and most of the old bars in the neighborhood have given way to establishments catering to younger crowds. When the workday ends at 5:00 p.m., people leave the area rather than remain for drinks, dinner, or just to window-shop. Parking and traffic remain the problems they were years ago, as the area is now more congested than ever before. There is little reason to spend an evening in Oakland.

Although many changes have taken place in the area, Oakland is not a ghost town. Rather, it is an extremely busy place during weekdays. Thousands of people visit their doctors in Oakland, and others utilize the university's academic and research facilities. While several noteworthy organizations and groups have left Oakland, the services provided by the University of Pittsburgh have been invaluable. The medical center has been a savior to many residents of Allegheny County, and the University has shaped many of the region's young minds. Today's Oakland is vastly different than yesterday's, but the area continues to benefit Pittsburghers in other ways.

Still, fans cling to their memories of what was once Oakland's greatest attraction. Forbes Field was replaced by Three Rivers Stadium, a concrete building that was part of a nationwide trend to build multi-purpose facilities. At first hailed as a grand success, Three Rivers is now recognized as a failure. Its seats are too far from the playing field, destroying the intimacy between players and fans that made Forbes Field so special. Its surface is artificial, and baseballs bounce more directly off it than they did when small stones filled the basepaths at Forbes Field. There are a few places to go before and after games to eat, drink, or simply stroll, just like in Oakland. There is no park in the background at which fans can gaze, but only a sea of empty seats. Clearly, Three Rivers Stadium lacks the ambiance of Forbes Field.

The poor quality of Three Rivers Stadium, combined with the trend in baseball to return to smaller, baseball-only parks, has created a desire in Pittsburgh to build such a facility. People yearn for another Forbes Field, and some still wonder why it was lost and if it could survive today. If David Lawrence and his Renaissance planners had not called for a new stadium, and if Edward Litchfield had not deemed the acquisition of Forbes Field as crucial to Pitt's expansion and survival, we may have found out for ourselves. Even though these events did occur, fans cite Fenway Park in Boston and Wrigley Field in Chicago. These classic parks in crowded cities remain popular despite the development around them, as examples of the possibility that Forbes Field could still exist today. Could Forbes Field, if remodelled, have survived in Oakland, even with the growth of the University? Probably not, because the loss of streetcars and the switch of Forbes and Fifth Avenue to one-way streets in the 1970s would have made Oakland too crowded. The area is too small to accommodate adequate parking facilities, a necessary consideration given that most fans drive to games today. Perhaps a ballpark similar in its features to Forbes Field could exist in a more open area, but not in Oakland today.

Very few people in Oakland remember it as a different neighborhood. Some of those who linger are still hopeful that Oakland can once again become a special place, where everybody knows each other, where crime does not exist, and where no one ever leaves the area because everything they need is just a short walk away. They yearn for a place where people can gather, leave their worries behind, and bask in the natural beauty of their surroundings. Such a place was Forbes Field, but Forbes Field is gone now, and with it has gone the Oakland they loved. Still, one Oakland resident and proprietor remains positive about the area's return to glory. "I expect the neighborhood to bounce back after all the renovations and construction dies down," he says. "It may even be better than it was before[121]." Oakland used to be a place to reside, work, and enjoy life. Now, it is a place to learn and to heal.

This change is called progress, but perhaps progress isn't always such a wonderful concept.

CHAPTER NOTES

Chapter 1

1 Fintor, Craig, "One Man's Dedication: The Barney Dreyfuss Story," (Pittsburgh) North Star, June 13, 1977, p.16, 21.

2 Ibid.

3 Smizik, Bob, The Pittsburgh Pirates: An Illustrated History, (New York:

Walker and Company, 1990), p.7.

4 Smizik, The Pittsburgh Pirates, p.8.

5 "Barney Dreyfuss," The Sporting News, July 6, 1944.

6 Ibid.

7 Fintor, Pittsburgh North Star, p.21. The following description of the life of Barney Dreyfuss is based on information in this article.

8 The Sporting News, July 6, 1944.

9 Lieb, Frederick, The Pittsburgh Pirates, (New York: G.P. Putnam and Sons, 1949). The following description of Pirate history is based on information in Lieb's book.

10 Smizik, Bob, The Pittsburgh Pirates: An Illustrated History, (New York: Walker & Company, 1990), p.17, 18. The following description of Pirate history is based on pages 17and 18 of this book.

Chapter 2

11 Archives of Industrial Society, Hillman Library, University of

Pittsburgh, Pittsburgh, PA.

12 Ibid.

13 Couvares, Francis G., The Remaking of Pittsburgh: Class and Culture in an Industrializing City 1877-1919, (Albany: The State University of New York Press, 1984), p.32.

14 Smith, Katherine, Carnegie Magazine, "The Race for Schenley Park," October 1967, p.269.

15 Couvares, The Remaking of Pittsburgh, p.105.

16 Smith, "The Race for Schenley Park," p.269.

17 Ibid, p.271.

18 "A Plan for Pittsburgh's Cultural District, Oakland," (Pittsburgh

Regional Planning Association, 1961), p.10.

19 Toker, Franklin, Pittsurgh: An Urban Portrait, (University Park: Pennsylvania State University Press, 1986), p.81.

20 Ibid, p.103.

21 Alberts, Robert, Pitt: The Story of the University of Pittsburgh, 1787-

1987, (Pittsburgh: University of Pittsburgh Press, 1986), p.57.

22 Gigler, Rich, "Revisiting the Schenley," The Pittsburgh Press Roto,

April 18, 1982, p.32.

23 Toker, Pittsburgh, p.81.

24 Alberts, Pitt, p.57.

25 Ibid

26 Toker, Pittsburgh, p.120.

27 Alberts, Pitt, p.57.

28 Toker, Pittsburgh, p.80.

29 The Official Baseball Dope Book, (The Sporting News, 1983), p.85.

30 Lieb, Frederick, The Pittsburgh Pirates, (New York: G. P. Putnam and

Sons, 1949), p.131.

Chapter 3

31 Bonk, Daniel L., "Ballpark Figures: The Story of Forbes Field," Pittsburgh History Magazine, (Pittsburgh: Historical Society of Western Pennsylvania, Summer 1993), p.55.

32 Keck, Harry, Pittsburgh Sun-Telegraph, December 3, 1958, p.25.

33 Lancaster, Donald G., "Forbes Field Praised as a Gem When It Opened,"

 Baseball Research Journal, Volume 15, p.26. and Pittsburgh Gazette-Times

October 18, 1908, p.7.

34 Lancaster, "Forbes Field," p.26.

35 Bonk, "Ballpark Figures," p.56.

36 Lancaster, "Forbes Field," p.26-28. The description of the grandstand, the bleachers, the other amenities of the ballpark, and the opening game is based on information in this article.

37 Lancaster, "Forbes Field,", p.28, and Pittsburgh Press, March 1, 1909.

38 Bonk, "Ballpark Figures," p.65.

39 Ibid.

40 Pittsburgh Press, June 30, 1909, p.2.

41 Smizik, Bob, The Pittsburgh Pirates: An Illustrated History, (New York: Walker and Company, 1990), p.19.

42 Bonk, "Ballpark Figures," p.65.

Chapter 4

43 Toker, Franklin, Pittsburgh: An Urban Portrait, (University Park: Pennsylvania State University Press, 1986), p.121.

44 Alberts, Robert, Pitt: The Story of the University of Pittsburgh, 1787-1987, (Pittsburgh: University of Pittsburgh Press, 1986), p.62.

45 Alberts, Pitt, p.70.

46 Ibid, p.85

47 Ibid, p.92.

48 Brown, Mark M., "The Cathedral of Learning: Concept, Design, Construction," (March 1987, Department of News and Publications, University of Pittsburgh).

49 Ibid., p.18.

50 Alberts, Pitt, p.115.

51 Ibid. p.118.

52 Ibid., p.119.

53 McHugh, Roy, "Oakland: Yesterday, Today, Tonight," The Pittsburgh Press Roto, May 4, 1975, p.9.

54 Heineman, Kenneth J., "The Changing Face of Schenley Park," Pittsburgh History, Fall'89 edition, Volume 72, Number 3, p. 115.

Chapter 5

55 Smizik, Bob, The Pittsburgh Pirates: An Illustrated History, (New York: Walker and Company, 1990), p.22.

56 Ibid., p.25.

57 Interview with Art McKennan, Pittsburgh, PA, August 13, 1994.

58 Interview with Stu Qualiey, Pittsburgh, PA, December 30, 1994.

59 Smizik, The Pittsburgh Pirates, p.30

60 Ibid., p.31.

61 Lieb, Frederick, The Pittsburgh Pirates, (New York: G. P. Putnam and Sons, 1949), p.203

62 Interview with Stu Qualiey, Pittsburgh, PA, December 30, 1994.

63 Smizik, The Pittsburgh Pirates, p.34.

64 Ibid.

65 Interview with Art McKennan, Pittsburgh, PA, August 13, 1994.

66 McHugh, Roy, "Oakland: Yesterday, Today, Tonight, "Pittsburgh Press Roto, May 4, 1975, p.7.

67 Smizik, The Pittsburgh Pirates, p.37. The following description of Pirate history is based on Smizik's book.

68 Smith, Curt. Voices of the Game, (New York: Simon & Schuster, 1987), p,75.

69 Ibid.

70 Ibid., p.76.

71 Pittsburgh Pirate Press Release, January 30, 1940.

72 Ward, Geoffrey C. and Burns, Ken. Baseball: An Illustrated History. (New York, Alfred A. Knopf, 1994), p.276-278.

Chapter 6

73 Smizik, Bob. The Pittsburgh Pirates: An Illustrated History, (New York: Walker & Company, 1990), p.67.

74 Ibid.

75 Interview with Tom Johnson, Pittsburgh, PA, January 7, 1995.

76 Ibid.

77 O'Brien, Jim, Maz and the Sixty Bucs, (Pittsburgh: James P. O'Brien Publishing, 1993), p.211.

78 Smizik, The Pittsburgh Pirates, p.71.

79 Interview with Joey Diven, Pittsburgh, PA, January 10, 1995.

80 Interview with Roy McHugh, Pittsburgh, PA, December 30, 1995.

81 Ibid.

82 Ibid.

83 Interview with Larry Dash, Pittsburgh, PA, August 11, 1994, and Interview with Joey Diven, Brookline, PA, January 10, 1995.

84 Interview with Roy McHugh.

85 Interview with Joe O'Toole, Pittsburgh, PA, January 9, 1995.

86 Interview with Joey Diven.

87 Ibid.

88 O'Brien, Maz and the '60 Bucs, p.362.

89 Interview Roy McHugh.

90 Pittsburgh Press, May 10, 1982.

91 Interview with Tom Johnson.

92 Smizik, The Pittsburgh Pirates, p.76.

Chapter 7

93 Alberts, Robert, Pitt: The Story of the University of Pittsburgh, 1787-1987, (Pittsburgh: University of Pittsburgh Press, 1987), p.198.

94   University Archives, Board of Trustees Minutes, Hillman Library, University of Pitsburgh, October 14, 1947.

95   University Archives, Executive Committee of the Board of Trustees Minutes, Hillman Library, University of Pittsburgh, May 31, 1951.

96   Alberts, Pitt, p.263-264. The following description of Pitt's expansion projects, specifically the acquisitions of the Schenley Apartments, the Schenley Hotel, and the Ruskin Apartments, is based on information from these pages.

97 University Archives, Board of Trustees Minutes, University of Pittsburgh, Hillman Library, March 12, 1957.

98 University Archives, Board of Trustees Minutes, University of Pittsburgh, Hillman Library, June 16, 1958.

99   University Archives, Executive Committee Meeting of the Board of Trustees Minutes, University of Pittsburgh, Hillman Library, March 19, 1958, p.303.

100   Library and Archives, Historical Society of Western Pennsylvania, Pittsburgh, PA. ACCD/Three Rivers Collection, Municipal Sports Center, Preliminary Report, April 1957., p.2.

101   Archives of Industrial Society, Hillman Library, University of Pittsburgh, Report on the proposed new stadium, Introduction.

102   Archives of Industrial Society, Hillman Library, University of Pittsburgh, Stanton Belfour Oral History Collection of the Pittsburgh Renaissance Project of the University of Pittsburgh, Interview with Dr. William McClelland, August 15, 1973.

103 University Archives, Minutes of the Meeting of the Board of Trustees, University of Pittsburgh, Hillman Library, June 10, 1958, p.321.

104 University Archives, Minutes of the Executive Committee Meeting of the Board of Trustees, University of Pittsburgh, Hillman Library, November 13, 1958, p.89.

Chapter 8

105 Interview with Roy McHugh, Pittsburgh, PA, December 30, 1994, and Interview with Art McKennan, Pittsburgh, PA, August 13, 1994.

106 Smizik, Bob, The Pittsburgh Pirates: An Illustrated History, (New York: Walker & Company, 1990), p.98.

107 O'Brien, Jim, Maz and the Sixty Bucs, (Pittsburgh: James P. O'Brien Publishing, 1993), p.129.

108 Ibid.

109 Interview with Art McKennan, Pittsburgh, PA, August 13, 1994.

110 Smizik, The Pittsburgh Pirates, p.104.

111 Sindler, Mark A., The Pitt News, August 31, 1984.

112 Smizik, The Pittsburgh Pirates, p.104.

113 Ibid, p.105.

114 O'Brien, Maz and the '60 Bucs, p.106.

115 Smizik, The Pittsburgh Pirates, p.107.

116 Archives of Industrial Society, University of Pittsburgh, Hillman Library, Stanton Belfour Oral

History Collection of the Pittsburgh Renaissance Project, Interview with Dr. William McClelland.

Chapter 9

117 Ibid.

118 Alberts, Robert, Pitt: The Story of the University of Pittsburgh, 1787-1987, (Pittsburgh: University of Pittsburgh Press, 1986), p. 319.

119 Interview with Dr. Jack Freeman, Philadelphia, PA, January 23, 1995.

120 McHugh, Roy, "Oakland: Yesterday, Today, Tonight," The Pittsburgh Press Roto, May 4, 1975, p.9.

Epilogue

121 Fanzo, Michael, "Oakland", The Observer, March 1995, p.18.

List of Interviews

Date:	Interviewee:
August 9, 1994	Mr. Daniel Bonk
August 13, 1994	Mr. Arthur McKennan
August 16, 1994	Ms. Sally O'Leary
August 20, 1994	Ms. Ruth Lavallee
August 22, 1994	Mr. Larry Dash
August 28, 1994	Dr. Wesley Posvar
November 14, 1994	Mr. Charlie Feeney
December 28, 1994	Mr. Dan Rooney
December 30, 1994	Mr. Roy McHugh
December 30, 1994	Mr. Stu Quailey
January 9, 1995	Mr. Joseph O'Toole
January 10, 1995	Mr. Joey Diven
January 10, 1995	Mr. Peter Demarest
January 13, 1995	Mr. Thomas Johnson
January 23, 1995	Dr. Jack Freeman

CRITICAL BIBLIOGRAPHY

NOTE:

The following is intended to serve as a guide to the research I have conducted for my thesis. It will have two purposes: 1) to present to the readers of my thesis a categorized list and description of my most valuable sources, and 2) to provide anyone who wishes to pursue further my work with a solid foundation. I have highlighted (in boldface) the sources that were most useful to me and discussed why they were beneficial. Anyone interested in conducting research on the history of a building and its surroundings should find this essay to be of some assistance.

PRIMARY SOURCES

Memoirs and Published Correspondence:

This material was particularly helpful in gaining a thorough understanding of the sale of Forbes Field in 1958, the events that led up to the sale, and the plan for a new stadium. The Archives of Industrial Society at the University of Pittsburgh's Hillman Library (hereinafter referred to as AIS) has an extensive collection of materials covering the Pittsburgh Renaissance project, a comprehensive upgrading of the city that took place over several years immediately after World War II. The growth of the Renaissance is directly related to the growth of the University of Pittsburgh and the decline of Oakland as the city's sports center.

The AIS is home to a special collection, entitled "Pittsburgh Renaissance Project: The Stanton Belfour Oral History Collection." It contains a living record of the Pittsburgh Renaissance, obtained from the oral reminiscences of prominent Pittsburgh citizens, on both cassettes and transcripts. Among those most helpful were interviews with Mayor Joseph Barr, Park Martin, Gwilym A. Price, and Dr. William McClelland. These transcripts provided me with information about the Renaissance and its effects from the perspectives of politicians, Pittsburgh's elite, and the University of Pittsburgh.

While these two sources are helpful, neither is as insightful or as important as the Report on Proposed New Stadium, prepared by the Joint City-County Stadium Study Committee (also available at AIS). In this thirty-seven-page report, the committee outlines the need for a new stadium, identifies potential locations for the new stadium, and explores the financial options available for either refurbishing an existing stadium or constructing a new one. Page 5 of the report clearly explains Oakland's size inadequacies for sports, page 6 discusses specific traffic and parking problems around Forbes Field, and page 12 details the liabilities that the city/county would incur if either Pitt Stadium or Forbes Field were renovated to become a true multi-purpose facility. The report also contains maps of the new stadium and its surrounding area. The recommendations made in this report in 1958 were followed in many ways.

Another revealing source concerning the demise of Forbes Field is found in the University Archives of Hillman Library (herein referred to as UA). The UA's most helpful sources are the minutes of the University's Board of Trustees meetings, as well as the minutes of the Board's Executive Committee meetings. The Executive Committee meeting on November 13, 1958 (Pages 88-93) marks Chancellor Litchfield's initial proposal for the University to purchase the site of Forbes Field. The minutes of the November 19, 1958, joint meeting of the Executive Committee and the Physical Site and Development Committee provide further details of Litchfield's proposal. The minutes of the December 9, 1958, meeting of the Board of Trustees contain the official proposal and resolution by the board to purchase

Forbes Field. Other meetings of note include the Board's meeting on March 3, 1958, the Executive Committee's meetings on February 11, 1958, and March 19, 1958, the Board's meeting on June 10, 1958, and the Executive Committee's meeting on June 16, 1958. These meetings included discussions of, among other things, the use of the field by the Pittsburgh Steelers football team, the leasing of the field to the Pirates, and the possibility of University teams playing at Forbes Field. The most intriguing set of minutes is from the April 2, 1959, meeting of the Board, where Chancellor Litchfield addresses the proposal to convert the University's stadium into a municipal stadium. Pages 266-284 of those minutes document Litchfield's opposition to such a plan.

Graphic Materials:

There are several graphic items that provide key insights into the subject, particularly because many of the relevant structures are no longer in existence. Sally O'Leary of the Pittsburgh Pirates permitted me to view every photograph of Forbes Field that the Pirates have in their collection. These photos allowed me to see the park from various angles, both during games and at idle times. The pictures were a tremendous supplement to the raving about Forbes Field's beauty that I had continuously heard. The closeness to the field of the seats, as well as the enormous dimensions of the park, are visible in the Pirates' pictures, many of which I have obtained prints of, which can be found throughout my thesis.

The Pennsylvania Department of the Carnegie Library of Pittsburgh (herein referred to as PA-CLP) has a small collection of photos of Forbes Field, as well as one of the Oakland buildings. In particular, picture A 1114 (in the Forbes Field file) gives an incredible view of Forbes Field in its inaugural year. This picture should be compared to picture B 553, which was taken after 1925, and thus shows the right-field stands that had since been added. There are also several noteworthy photos of the Oakland area at AIS.

To gain an understanding of the field's initial placement within the Oakland area and its subsequent development, the Plate maps at PA-CLP were most helpful. The 1904 book, plates 18-20, shows the Carnegie Library, the Schenley Hotel, and other structures that would soon become neighbors to Forbes Field. These plates also allowed me to understand how truly large the Schenley Estate was, as it occupied almost all of Oakland. The 1914 book, plates 19 & 23-25, showed the addition of Forbes Field on Bouquet and Louisa streets, and the division of Schenley's estate into a park as well as an area for fine homes. Finally, the 1923 book gives the impression that Forbes was no longer simply a field in the midst of a public park. Additions to the area included the Schenley Theatre, the Schenley Apartments, and the Steel City Auto Company (under Forbes Field on Pennant Place). These 1923 maps display the tremendous increase in the number of buildings of the University of Pittsburgh, just north of Forbes Field on Fifth Avenue.

Another "graphic" source helped me to understand the changes occurring in Oakland from 1950-1970. The City Directories, located at the PA-CLP, list the proprietors/residents of all properties within the city. By examining these directories, it is easy to notice the changes that occurred in Oakland, particularly within a 10-block radius on Forbes Street. Most remarkable is the influx of medical offices and University of Pittsburgh buildings, accompanied by a decrease in local stores, in what was once a thriving business district.

Interviews:

Due to the fact that I was never so fortunate as to see Forbes Field as a complete structure (part of its outfield wall remains in its original location), it has been necessary to question others about details of the park and its surroundings. On August 13, 1994, I had the pleasure of meeting Art McKennan, a Pirates employee from 1919 to 1986, at his home. Mr. McKennan was born in 1905 and grew up near Forbes Field. Our conversation was very revealing, covering old players, anecdotes, the beauty of the park, concessions at the field, transportation and parking problems, and other topics. He is a wonderful man and was a self-proclaimed "baseball rat" as a young man, which gave him incredible knowledge about Forbes Field, the Pirates, and Oakland in its early years.

In January 1995, I interviewed Tom Johnson in his office at the Pittsburgh law firm of Kirpatrick & Lockhart. Mr. Johnson was part-owner of the Pirates from 1946 to 1986, and was very knowledgeable about the history of Forbes Field since the Second World War. His perspective on the sale of Forbes Field to the University of Pittsburgh was unique and essential to my understanding of the sale. His comments were extremely revealing and more believable than any other scenario I had previously encountered involving reasons for the sale. When I confirmed his explanation for the sale with other sources, I was confident that it was correct and had based some of my interpretation of the sale on Mr. Johnson's words.

On January 23, 1995, I interviewed Dr. Jack Freeman in his office at the University of Pennsylvania. Dr. Freeman is currently the Acting Executive Vice President of Penn and has held various similar positions under Chancellor Wesley Posvar at the University of Pittsburgh from 1968 to the 1980s. Dr. Freeman explained the reasons for the delay in the destruction of Forbes Field and the effect of Pitt's expansion on the community. Again, his perspective was unique because he was the University's most important liaison to the community. The interview was revealing and supported many of the details one discovered in my interview with Dr. Posvar on August 28, 1994.

SECONDARY SOURCES

Books:

The previously mentioned primary sources would be of little use without a strong background in the histories of several key areas. I have read many books on these various histories, and in order to describe the relevance of each to my thesis, I have taken the liberty of dividing the category of "Books" into more specific categories.

1) Pittsburgh Baseball Histories

Although several books about the history of the Pittsburgh Pirates, such as Fred Lieb's and Jim O'Brien's, are excellent, Bob Smizik surpasses them's more thorough and modern team history entitled The Pittsburgh Pirates: An Illustrated History (New York: Walker & Co., 1990). As is suggested by the title, Smizik's book contains many more pictures of players than Lieb's. The other major difference between the two is that Smizik's book covers the history of the team well past the move from Forbes Field to Three Rivers Stadium. Its early history provides many insights into player-management relations, and the book has been my main source of information on the Pirates from 1947 to the modern era.

Another book that has been important to the development of my conception of baseball in Pittsburgh is Curt Smith's Voices of the Game.

(New York: Simon & Schuster, 1987) a history of broadcasting in baseball. This book discusses at length the careers of two great Pirate broadcasters, Rosey Rosewell and Bob Prince, and describes their effects on the baseball fans of Pittsburgh. This book is critical to understanding the value of broadcasting to baseball and its effect on the game, both in Pittsburgh and across the country.

2) Pittsburgh History

Several books present information about Pittsburgh and its physical history. These books have enabled me to understand the growth and development of Oakland, both as a distinct neighborhood and as part of the larger city of Pittsburgh. Franklin Toker's Pittsburgh: An Urban Portrait. (Penn State University Press, 1986) gives an excellent description of the history of Oakland's buildings and the growth of Oakland as Pittsburgh's cultural center.

3) University of Pittsburgh Growth

It is sufficient to read only one book for information on this topic. Robert C. Alberts' major work, The Story of the University of Pittsburgh. 1787-1987 (University of Pittsburgh Press, 1986) is an enormously informative book that provides a detailed history of the University. It is essential to obtain an understanding of the University's changing role within the city and the Oakland community. Although much of the information in this 450-page book may seem irrelevant, it contains important background details that enable one to understand the reasons behind the ultimate clash between education (the University) and athletics (Forbes Field) in Oakland.

Magazines:

Donald Lancaster's article, "Forbes Field Praised as a Gem when it Opened", appeared in the Baseball Research Journal, Volume 15. It is the most comprehensive history of Forbes Field's construction and the opening game there in existence. Although it is only four pages long, it provided me with many items from which I could conduct further research. It is extremely detailed, and its sources are mainly newspaper accounts of the day. Dan Bonk's article, which appeared in the Summer 1993 edition of Pittsburgh History, is also worth reading, but it is based largely on Lancaster's work.

Conclusion:

The above list and description of the sources I have used for my research on Forbes Field and the history of Oakland are not the only sources I have encountered. They are simply the ones that have been most valuable and pertinent to my work. It is my hope that through my brief account of these sources, the conclusions I draw about Forbes Field and its significance to the Oakland community will be better understood.

SELECTED BIBLIOGRAPHY

Primary Sources

Magazines:

Benswanger, William E. "Professional Baseball in Pittsburgh." Western Pennsylvania History Magazine, Volume 30, March-June 1947.

Published Reports:

Report of the Executive Committee of the Board of Trustees of the University of Pittsburgh: University of Pittsburgh, 31 May, 1951.

Report of the Executive Committee of the Board of Trustees of the University of Pittsburgh: University of Pittsburgh, 14 June, 1955.

Report to the Board of Trustees of the University of Pittsburgh: By Dr. Edward Litchfield, Chancellor. University of Pittsburgh, 12 December, 1955.

Report to the Board of Trustees of the University of Pittsburgh: By Dr. Edward

Litchfield, Chancellor. University of Pittsburgh, 18 January, 1956.

Report to the Board of Trustees of the University of Pittsburgh: By Dr. Edward Litchfield, Chancellor. University of Pittsburgh, 12 March, 1957.

Report to the Board of Trustees of the University of Pittsburgh: By Dr. Edward Litchfield, Chancellor. University of Pittsburgh, 11 February, 1958.

Report to the Board of Trustees of the University of Pittsburgh: By Dr. Edward Litchfield, Chancellor. University of Pittsburgh, 11 March, 1958.

Report to the Board of Trustees of the University of Pittsburgh: By Dr. Stanton Crawford, Secretary. University of Pittsburgh, 19 March, 1958.

Report to the Board of Trustees of the University of Pittsburgh: By Dr. Edward Litchfield, Chancellor. University of Pittsburgh, 10 June, 1958.

Report to the Board of Trustees of the University of Pittsburgh: By Dr. Edward Litchfield, Chancellor. University of Pittsburgh, 16 June, 1958.

Report of the Executive Committee of the Board of Trustees of the University of Pittsburgh: By Dr. Edward Litchfield, Chancellor. University of Pittsburgh, 13 November, 1958.

Report to the Board of Trustees of the University of Pittsburgh: By Dr. Edward Litchfield, Chancellor. University of Pittsburgh, 19 November, 1958.

Report on the Municipal Sports Center: By the Municipal Sports Center Çollaborative and Carnegie Instiute of Technology. April, 1957.

Report on the Conversion of Pitt Stadium into the Municipal Stadium: By Thomas Hamilton. University of Pittsburgh.

Report on Proposed New Stadium: By the Joint City-County Stadium Study Committee. September 1, 1958.

Published Interviews:

McClelland, William. "An Oral Interview with William McClelland." Transcript. Stanton Belfour Oral History Collection of the Pittsburgh Renaissance Project of the University of Pittsburgh. 15 August, 1973.

Montgomery, Edison. "An Oral Interview with Edison Montgomery." Interview by Lawrence Howard. Transcript. Stanton Belfour Oral History Collection of the Pittsburgh Renaissance Project of the University of Pittsburgh. 29 May, 1975.

Price, Gwilym A. "An Oral Interview with Gwilym Price." Transcript. Stanton Belfour Oral History Collection of the Pittsburgh Renaissance Project of the University of Pittsburgh. 23 May, 1975.

Starrett, Agnes and C.V. Starrett. "An Oral Interview Interview with Agnes and C.V. Starrett." Interview by Lawrence Howard and David Kurtzman. Transcript. Stanton Belfour Oral History Collection of the Pittsburgh Renaissance Project of the University of Pittsburgh. 10 May, 1972.

Newspapers:

Harper's Weekly, 22 May, 1909.

Oaklander, 20 April, 1911.

Oaklander, 11 May, 1911.

Oaklander, 1 June, 1911.

Pittsburgh Bulletin, 3 July, 1909.

Pittsburgh Dispatch Times, 18 July, 1909.

Pittsburgh Gazette Times, 18 October, 1908.

Pittsburgh Leader, 23 October, 1904.

Pittsburgh Press, 3 January, 1909.

Pittsburgh Press, 28 February, 1909.

Pittsburgh Press, 1 March, 1909.

Pittsburgh Press, 3 March, 1909.

Pittsburgh Press, 7 March, 1909.

Pittsburgh Press, 14 March, 1909.

Pittsburgh Press, 28 March, 1909.

Pittsburgh Press, 23 May, 1909.

Pittsburgh Press, 6 June, 1909.

Pittsburgh Press, 27 June, 1909.

Pittsburgh Press, 30 June, 1909.

Pittsburgh Press, 26 September, 1960.

Pittsburgh Press, 28 June, 1970.

Pittsburgh Press, 13 June 1975.

Secondary Sources

Pamphlets:

Brown, Mark M. The Cathedral of Learning: Concept, Design, Construction.

March 1987.

Books:

Alberts, Robert C. Pitt: The Story of the University of Pittsburgh, 1787-1987. Pittsburgh: University of Pittsburgh Press, 1986.

Alberts, Robert C. The Shaping of the Point. Pittsburgh: University of Pittsburgh

Press, 1980.

Benson, Michael. Ballparks of North America. Jefferson: McFarland & Company,

1989.

Couvares, Francis G. The Remaking of Pittsburgh: Class and Culture in an

Industrializing City, 1877-1919. Albany: State University of New York Press, 1984.

Kavanagh, Jack. Honus Wagner. New York: Chelsea House Publishers, 1994.

Kuklick, Bruce. To Every Thing A Season: Shibe Park and Urban Philadelphia, 1909-1976. Princeton: Princeton University Press, 1991.

Lieb, Frederick. The Pittsburgh Pirates. New York: G.P. Putnam & Sons, 1948.

Lowry, Phillip J. Green Cathedrals. Addison Wesley Company, 1992.

Murdock, Eugene. Baseball Betwen the Wars: Memories of the Game By the Men

 Who Played It. Westport, CT: Meckler Publishing, 1992.

Westport, CT: Meckler Publishing, 1991.

O'Brien, Jim. Maz and The '60 Bucs. Pittsburgh: James P. O'Brien Publsihing, 1993.

Official Baseball Dope Book. Craig Carter, Ed. St Louis: The Sporting News, 1983.

Ritter, Lawrence S. Lost Ballparks. New York: Penguin Books, 1992.

The Glory of Their Times. The Story of the Early Days ofBaseball By the Men Who Played It. New York: MacMillan Co., 1966.

Robinson, George, and Charles Salzberg. On A Clear Day, They Could See Seventh Place. New York: Dell Publishing.

Ruck, Rob. Sandlot Seasons: Sport in Black Pittsburgh, Chicago: University of Illinois Press, 1993.

Seymour, Harold. Baseball: The Golden Age, Volume II. New York: Oxford University Press, 1971.

Shannon, Bill, and George Kalinsky. The Ballparks. New York: Hawthorne Books,

1975.

Smith, Curt. Voices of the Game. New York: Fireside, Simon & Schuster, 1987.

Smizik, Bob. The Pittsburgh Pirates: An Illustrated History. New York: Walker & Company, 1990.

Toker, Franklin. Pittsburgh, An Urban Portrait. University Park, PA: Pennsylvania State University Press, 1986.

Van Trump, James D., and Arthur P. Ziegler, Jr. Landmark Architecture of Allegheny County. Pittsburgh History and Landmarks Foundation, 1967.

Ward, Geoffrey C., and Ken Burns. Baseball: An Illustrated History. New York: Alfred A. Knopf, Inc., 1994.

Weber, Michael. Don't Call Me Boss: David L. Lawrence, Pittsburgh's Renaissance Mayor. Pittsburgh: University of Pittsburgh Press, 1988.

Magazines:

Bonk, Daniel L. "Ballpark Figures: The Story of Forbes Field." Pittsburgh History. Pittsburgh: Historical Society of Western Pennsylvania, Summer 1993.

McHugh, Roy. "Oakland: Yesterday, Today, Tonight." The Pittsburgh Press Roto.

Pittsburgh: Pittsburgh Press, 4 May, 1975.